Tales Along El Camino Sierra

David & Gayle Woodruff

David & Gayle Woodruff

El Camino Sierra Publishing
elcaminosierra395@gmail.com
1326 Kimmerling Rd # A
Gardnerville, NV 89460

ISBN-10:069268073X

ISBN-13:978-0692680735

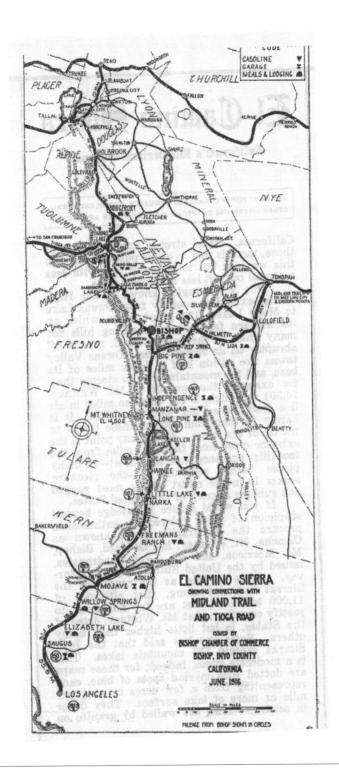

EL CAMINO SIERRA
SHOWING CONNECTIONS WITH
MIDLAND TRAIL
AND TIOGA ROAD
ISSUED BY
BISHOP CHAMBER OF COMMERCE
BISHOP, INYO COUNTY
CALIFORNIA
JUNE 1916

MILEAGE FROM BISHOP SHOWN IN CIRCLES

CONTENTS

1.	The Mountain Highway	1
2.	A Man for All Seasons	9
3.	Little Lake	13
4.	Terrifying Tioga	17
5.	Mammoth Mountain Man	21
6.	Apple Orchards and Internment	25
7.	Worth Saving	29
8.	Soaring to New Heights	33
9.	Lone Pine Ashram	37
10.	Skyway to the Mountains	41
11.	Irrepressible Charles Brown	45
12.	A Showplace for All Time	49
13.	Above All Others	53
14.	Bringing Life to the Desert	59
15.	Wedding of the Waters	63
16.	Dirty Sock	69
17.	Let's Have a Picnic	71
18.	Seemed Like a Good Idea	75

CONTENTS

19.	Steamships of Silver	79
20.	Not Where We Thought	83
21.	Anchors Aweigh...	87
22.	The Pack That Walked Like a Man	89
23.	Yellowstone in the Sierra	95
24.	Big Tree of Big Pine	99
25.	Owens Valley's Iron Horse	101
26.	Keough Hot Spring	105
27.	Sherwood Forest	107
28.	Fish On!	109
29.	Midland Trail	115
30.	Power to Bodie	117
31.	Mono Lake Memories	119
32.	I Feel the Earth Move	123
33.	Science at Extreme Heights	125
34.	Jewel of the Sierra	127
35.	Ski Independence	131
36.	The Red Fish	135

Front Cover Photo-El Camino Sierra (Highway 395) just north of Independence-California Department of Transportation. Copyright 1962 California Department of Transportation, all rights reserved.

ACKNOWLEDGEMENTS

There are always so many people that are involved in projects such as this that one becomes fearful important contributors will inadvertently be overlooked in the acknowledgments. That said, there is absolutely no way we could have accomplished this passion of ours without the assistance of our many dear relatives, friends, acquaintances and supporters.

Thank you to sister Karla Pierce for the hours spent tediously editing these many pages of text. This book could not have been completed without your invaluable help. Cris Chater's and Alyse Bertenthal's "second look" on our editing panel helped ensure what we hope is a well edited product. Huge amounts of gratitude to: Jon Klusmire, Roberta Harlan and Heather Todd from the Eastern California Museum in Independence (a must see by the way if you haven't already done so) for the time spent assisting us with research and numerous photographs; Elizabeth Glazner of Bishop who provided us professional help with our cover design; Florene Trainor and Kristin Noles from the California Department of Transportation Bishop office for helping us with additional research and photographs; Pam Vaughn from Laws Museum, David Carle from the Mono Basin Historical Society, Ray DeLea of www.owensvalleyhistory.com and the dozens of other folks who have provided us with information, insight and guidance. This has been the epitome of a group project and we are forever indebted to all.

The official dedication of El Camino Sierra took place along former Los Angeles mayor Fred Eaton's chicken ranch south of Big Pine on August 30, 1910. Eaton had improved about 1 ¼ miles of roadway running along his property, thus creating the first "improved" highway in the Eastern Sierra. California Governor Gillett presided over the dedication, which was sponsored by the Inyo Good Roads Club.

Travel along El Camino Sierra was slow going during its early years. Despite the road often being rough and dusty, the benefits of being linked to the outside world were apparent from the very start. Here's a view of the original highway, with the level of Mono Lake much higher than it is today.

A State of Mind

The Eastern Sierra has long been a place that holds a sentimental and romantic attraction to most of the people who visit, as well as those who are fortunate enough to live there. This certainly has been true for the two of us.

Perhaps nowhere else does scenery so sublime, present itself so magnificently and on such a grand scale as it does while traveling U.S. Highway 395 through Inyo and Mono Counties. For over 250 miles the mountains, forests and deserts combine to make a landscape so beautiful that one sometimes thinks only the imaginers and creators from a Hollywood movie studio could create a scene so perfect. A road trip here becomes the basis of what dreams are made of.

We both clearly remember our own dreams of upcoming visits to what author Mary Austin referred to as *The Land of Little Rain*. The anticipation of knowing we would soon be motoring on that special ribbon of black top known as three-ninety-five proved almost unbearable. We dreamed night and day of the many pleasures we knew this mythical highway would soon deliver us to. For us, Highway 395 became as much a state of mind as an avenue to adventure.

Becoming Eastern Sierra residents only increased its pull on the emotional strings of our hearts and minds. Being able to see the noble and brooding peaks, to take in the aroma of the sagebrush and pine and watch and listen to the dancing of the magical creeks and streams on a daily basis, further ingrained this enchanting byway in our psyche.

Over time, it became very clear that we were not alone in holding this highway in such sentimental and romantic regard. With near unanimity, our Eastern Sierra neighbors, our out-of-area friends and relatives, and visitors we would meet at work or on the trail - all seemed to share that same starry-eyed wonderment of "that road" they had traveled to so many special and enduring memories.

We listened to hundreds of people share their heartfelt reminiscence of their personal Highway 395 experiences. Most expressed their feelings in moving and often emotional reflection. It was clear this iconic roadway has led to the creation of lifelong remembrances with nearly all who have traveled it.

We began to think of those from the generations before us who have lived, traveled and vacationed along Highway 395. What were their stories? Were emotional ties to it as strong then as they are today?

The Highway 395 auto road got its start at the beginning of the 20th century, shortly after the invention of the first automobile and has played an instrumental part in the development of Inyo and Mono Counties ever since.

The Highway was dubbed El Camino Sierra-*The Mountain Highway* by its original conceptors before the first roadbed was even graded. These folks "dreamed" of a route that would make travel easier, enable more commerce and unveil to the world the glory that is the Eastern Sierra.

Ever since the first explorers and settlers passed along the base of the Sierra Nevada Mountains, an interesting and fascinating human history has been unfolding. *Tales Along El Camino Sierra* has taken just a few of the lesser known chapters of Eastern Sierra history and assembled them for Highway 395 enthusiasts to enjoy. Some of the tales are interesting, some unusual and all of them entertaining. It is our hope that while our readers create their own special memories in this enchanted land, they reflect upon the hard work and determination of all those who have come before.

"Difficult roads often lead us to the most beautiful destination."

CHAPTER ONE

THE MOUNTAIN HIGHWAY

The roads of Eastern California were not much more than improved wagon trails in 1909. The automobile had just been introduced to the American public less than a decade before. Despite its remote location in relation to the rest of the state, the Eastern slope of the Sierra Nevada Mountains had already seen the arrival of the horseless carriage.

Passable roadways in California barely existed, even in the urban areas at that time. Travel to the rural parts of the state was made only with the greatest of difficulty.

In 1909, the state legislature called for an $18 million-dollar bond issue to be presented to the state's voters for the purpose of acquiring and constructing a State Highway System. Governor James Gillett signed the act and the measure was scheduled to go to a vote of the people at the general election of November, 1910. It would be up to the people of the state to decide if they really wanted to have (and pay for) good roads.

The people of Inyo County wasted no time in making up their minds. Following the lead of the national *Good Roads* movement, community members came together in April of 1910, to formally launch the Inyo Good Roads Club.

The Club counted sixty-two members when it first organized. Perhaps most important among them was W. Gillette Scott, who held the office of Corresponding Secretary. History books credit Scott as having been the author of the name El Camino Sierra.

The name was applied to the proposed highway that the Club envisioned would run from Mojave, through Little Lake, Olancha, Lone Pine, Independence, Big Pine, Bishop, Lee Vining and Bridgeport, and on to the junction with the proposed new Sonora Pass Road.

Figure 1-This sign was placed along a 1 ¼ mile stretch of improved highway that former Los Angeles mayor Fred Eaton had worked on, that ran alongside his huge chicken ranch south of Big Pine. Copyright 1910, California Department of Transportation, all rights reserved.

The enthusiastic supporters conducted several workdays, doing what they could to improve the local roads by hand, to show the state they were serious when it came to getting their share of the highway bond funds.

They even made governor Gillett an honorary member of their Road Club and invited him to Inyo County to officially dedicate the new El Camino Sierra.

Impressed by the enthusiasm of the local boosters, Governor Gillett accepted their offer and made his way first to Lone Pine, and then Bishop, being the first governor of California known to have set foot in Inyo County. The highlight of the event was the unveiling of the metal plaque marking the first segment of the new route (see photograph on preceding page).

California voters passed that bond measure in 1910, though it was several years until the Eastern Sierra began to receive any of the funds. Nevertheless, Inyo Good Road Club members held steadfast in the promotion of their route, never missing an opportunity to get its name in the papers and in front of the State Highway Commission.

In 1911, it was announced that the Panama-Pacific International Exposition, the world's fair to commemorate the opening of the Panama Canal, would be held in San Francisco in 1915. An immediate flood of letters was received by the organizers, inquiring of the best way to see California by motorcar.

Seeing an opportunity of nearly unlimited proportions, Inyo Good Roads Scott suggested a grand route be promoted, to be known as the Pasear, a Spanish word meaning to "stroll and look about."

Scott suggested a route that would allow tourists to "take in the sublimity of the ocean, the desolation of the desert, the grandeur of the Sierra, and the fertility of the valleys: a combination of historic, scenic and natural attractions not equaled by any other highway in the world."

The route would take in four of California's principle (or at least most promoted) roads: El Camino Real, El Camino San Diego, El Camino Sierra and El Camino Capital.

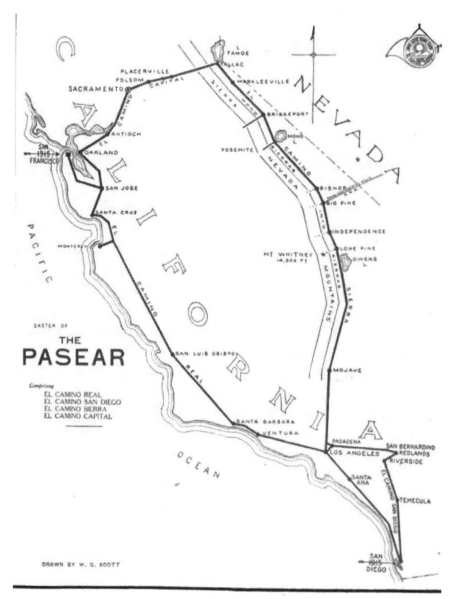

Figure 2- Map of the "Pasear" route proposed by Inyo Good Roads W. G. Scott.
A pilot tour of the route was organized by Scott, enlisting the sponsorship
of the Studebaker Motor Company, which provided four of their best
autos. The month-long trip covered almost two-thousand miles and
generated enormous publicity and interest. Sunset Magazine columnist
Peter Kyne wrote that, once completed, the El Camino Sierra would be
"the greatest automobile highway on earth." It seemed the great envisioned
roadway just might come about.

Figure 3- Inyo Good Roads Club promoting the Pasear Tour in Bishop, 1912.

Finally, in the fall of 1914, the state highway commission sent a survey party to the Eastern Sierra to assess the most critical road needs of the area. It didn't take long before the state began planning for project development. The grade up Sherwin Hill was determined to be the most urgent project requiring state highway funding in the Eastern Sierra.

It wasn't until the summer of 1916 that the difficult 3,000-foot climb from the floor of the Owens Valley to the top of Sherwin Hill (now Sherwin Grade) was finally surmounted and the first section of state highway in the Eastern Sierra was completed.

A celebration, the likes of which had never been seen in these parts, was planned to be held at a meadow near the top of Sherwin Hill. The event was held on September 5, 1916 with the Inyo Register proclaiming;

"EL CAMINO SIERRA'S FIRST UNIT WAS AUSPICIOUSLY DEDICATED."

The newspaper went on, "A thousand people shared the pleasure of an outing on Rock Creek under a cloudless sky...[a]celebration of first achievement in greatest undertaking for future development of all Eastern California."

This dedication was only the beginning of El Camino Sierra. Even though nearly six years had elapsed since the original highway bond measure was passed, the people of the Eastern Sierra had stood resolute in their commitment to bring better roads to their rural area. Work was already underway on more state highway projects in the Eastern Sierra and additional state highway bonds had been approved by the California voters.

Figure 4- Over one thousand people gathered to celebrate the completion of the first segment of El Camino Sierra, September 1916.

Over the next nine years, Inyo and Mono Counties would see improved roads built throughout their region. The efforts of the Inyo Good Road Club, and its indefatigable secretary W. Gillette Scott in particular, were now bringing rapid progress to the area's highway system.

As roads improved, so did interest in visiting the land of nature's paradise. The San Francisco Call pronounced, "It is doubtful if in any other community in all the world has the possibilities of an auto tour which would even approach the wonders of El Camino Sierra. One must see it for oneself." From sightseeing to fishing to hiking, tourism began to play a major role in the Eastern Sierra.

Boosters expanded the area to be covered by El Camino Sierra north to Lake Tahoe. Brochures were printed and advertising campaigns and promotions were undertaken by communities from Inyokern to Carson City.

California and its roadways grew exponentially. Bond measures to build more state roads were passed by the voters on almost a yearly basis. State highways were built over Tioga, Sonora, Ebbetts and Westgard Passes to connect to El Camino Sierra. It appeared the road would live on for time immortal.

But as time passed, so did the use of the name El Camino Sierra. Records are unclear as to why the disuse of the name came about. What is known however, is that the Los Angeles Aqueduct was completed in 1913, and the citizens of Inyo, and later Mono County, certainly had their hands full with numerous new concerns.

Businesses and residents alike saw more and more land and its water rights become property of the city of Los Angeles. Most people in Inyo became focused on surviving economically, as businesses closed and neighbors moved away. Promotion and celebration was probably not on the minds of most.

In the 1930s, the federal government was expanding its own highway system. Incorporating state highways and building new roads in some areas, U.S. Highway 395 was officially designated, extending from the Canadian border in Washington State, to the Mexican border near San Diego.

Little mention of the name El Camino Sierra is found in records since this time. "Three-ninety-five" had an easy flow to it and the mountain highway soon took on this new sobriquet.

Tales Along El Camino Sierra takes a look at some of the people, places and events that in one way or another have been affected by, or had an effect upon, this grand roadway over the years.

Many highways have generated an interest and special attraction from those that use them and the lives they affect. Highway 395-El Camino Sierra seems to take that special attraction to the highest level.

This special roadway has been a part of the dreams of millions who have followed its ribbon of blacktop. A magical weekend making fresh tracks on the powder, a never to be forgotten fishing trip, a life changing experience while hiking among the jagged Sierra peaks, or the two-week vacation that creates enduring memories that will last a lifetime…these are the images and tales of El Camino Sierra.

Figure 5-Celebrating completion of paved road from Bishop to Mojave-1931.
Figure 5A--(below) El Camino Sierra in Round Valley, Copyright 1959 California Department of Transportation, all rights reserved.

CHAPTER TWO

A MAN FOR ALL SEASONS

It seems only fitting that a land of such grand scale as the Eastern Sierra draws men and women of equal stature. Father John J. Crowley, the Desert Padre as many called him, stood as a giant of a man among all who knew him.

Born in Ireland, Father Crowley moved to southern California to begin his priesthood shortly after graduating from College of the Holy Cross in Massachusetts in 1918. Soon after his arrival, the Archbishop asked for a volunteer to become the Catholic priest for California's "desert" area. Young Crowley immediately stepped up for the assignment.

His parish covered the area from Bishop to Death Valley. Crowley wrote, "With such an expanse of territory it was out of the question to try and establish a headquarters, and thus I gained the enviable reputation of being an 'ecclesiastical tramp,' covering a little more than 50,000 miles in a bit over a year."

Ministering in this expansive land with its lack of good roads was not for the faint of heart. Crowley went on, "Breakdowns of course, were to be expected, and delays, but having had the seat-back cut out for sleeping, I felt no qualms about being caught in the desert a hundred miles from nowhere, and many a hotel bill has been saved while I snored beneath the stars."

Crowley spent five years along El Camino Sierra before being transferred to Fresno's St. Johns Cathedral in 1924. He faithfully served the parishioners of the raisin capital for the next ten years. But all the while, Crowley kept the memory of his time in the desert close at hand. In 1934, Crowley returned to his beloved desert to be its cleric once more.

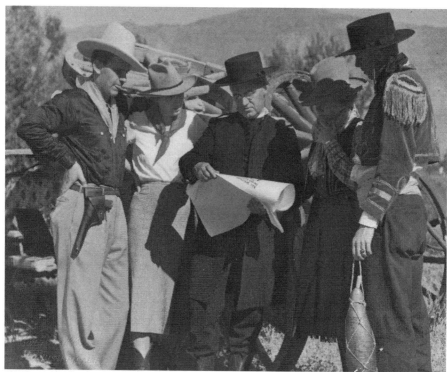

Figure 6- Father Crowley fit in well with his Eastern Sierra congregation.

Upon his return, Father Crowley was shocked by what he saw. After 21 years of water diversions by the Los Angeles Department of Water & Power (LADWP), the economic situation in Eastern California looked dismal. Many businesses had closed, many people had moved away, and the outlook for those that remained was very bleak.

Crowley believed his calling led him beyond just spreading the word of the gospel. Alarmed by the prevailing mood of utter despair exhibited by many, Crowley felt their economic exigency needed to be tended to as well as their spiritual needs. Father Crowley thought he might use his skills to lead his flock to the promised land of a tourism-based economy.

By the 1930s, LADWP had purchased most of the private land in the Owens Valley along with its water rights and there was very little land left to develop. But the mountains loomed large, the creeks ran swift (at least until they reached the Aqueduct) and the scenery was unmatched. Father Crowley felt tourism was the Eastern Sierra's salvation, and moreover, that he would be the one to bring it.

For the next six years, Father Crowley promoted the beauty and attractions of the Eastern Sierra as vigorously as a Barnum & Bailey huckster. His unabashed popularization of the area's scenic and natural attractions aroused the fervor among all who heard him. His success at marketing and promotion became something of a legend.

Father Crowley convinced the Inyo County Board of Supervisors to declare the opening day of fishing season a county holiday. The night before the opener, he would hold a "blessing of the fishing tackle" mass, where locals and visitors alike would line up to have their equipment receive a proper consecration.

Figure 7- Father Crowley blessing rods and reels at Opening Day of Fishing.

An avid outdoorsman himself, Father Crowley hiked to the top of Mt. Whitney, the highest peak in the lower 48 states, and once there, held what was the first and only Catholic mass on its summit.

Figure 8- Father Crowley preparing to celebrate mass on top of Mt. Whitney.

Father Crowley continued his tireless promotion of tourism in the Eastern Sierra. In 1937, he organized and executed one of the biggest celebrations ever held along El Camino Sierra. (More on that in Chapter 15.)

In 1940, while driving through the desert near Inyokern, Crowley struck a wayward steer. Father Crowley lost his life on the magical highway that led so many people to the land he so loved. But the fruits of his tireless efforts will live on forever…along El Camino Sierra.

CHAPTER THREE

LITTLE LAKE

Drivers of yesteryear were well familiar with the hotel, cafe and gas station located near the large body of water along Highway 395, about ten miles north of the Inyo County line. Little Lake Resort was a welcoming pit stop as well as a destination to thousands of travelers on El Camino Sierra for eight decades.

The beginning of the 20th century saw many bold and progressive men and women who tested themselves and their ideas on taking the country in a fast paced, forward moving direction.

Bill Bramlette was a water driller by profession, and a daring racecar driver by passion. In 1914, Bill drove a Cadillac in the Great Cactus Derby Los Angeles to Phoenix road race, and there was no road. He came to be known as the "Monarch of the Desert Trail."

Later that same year, Bill and his new wife Elvira made their way up the rutted and dusty facsimile of a road running along the base of the Sierra Nevada Mountains to a Yosemite vacation. Despite the difficult travel, Bill foresaw a great increase in highway traffic through the scenic region in the years to come, and saw an opportunity at Little Lake for a successful tourist stopover.

Bill and Elvira bought one thousand acres of land including Little Lake itself. The property included a store, café, saloon, post office and a small hotel that had operated for a few years.

Business was good from the very start. As more and more people stopped at Bramlette's Little Lake facilities, plans were made for a new hotel to replace the original one lost in a recent fire, and to expand his guest services.

Bill Bramlette was yet another Eastern Sierran that well understood the value of publicity. As his new hotel was nearing completion, Bramlette decided to challenge the current L.A. to Bishop speed record. He chose a stock 1920, Lincoln touring car as his auto of preference.

These types of races were often sponsored by civic groups, good road clubs and local governments. Undoubtedly, this was yet another opportunity for the Inyo Good Roads Club to help draw attention to newly created El Camino Sierra.

Bramlette, with his brother Tony as his co-pilot, made the 203-mile trip in a record setting 7 hours 24 minutes. It was reported that between Lone Pine and Bishop, there were thirty right-angle turns around farmlands, and that Bramlette rolled the big Lincoln onto its side near the Lone Pine Cemetery. Bystanders helped right the car.

Figure 9-Bill Bramlette (left standing) arrives in Bishop after his record setting run from L.A.

A crowd of hundreds welcomed Bramlette as he roared into Bishop. Newspaper columnists spread the story of the record setting trip on El Camino Sierra far and wide.

After the race, Bramlette returned to Little Lake to complete the construction of his hotel. The hotel was meant to be a showpiece, with many amenities built in to the new building. The lake was stocked with bass and for a time, public fishing was allowed.

The hotel and services became a landmark for travelers on El Camino Sierra. Little Lake became a very popular stop for fuel, food and lodging. Bill and Elvira dutifully cared for their constituency up until Bill's death in 1940.

Figure 10-(above) & 10A (below) At its peak, Little Lake boasted a hotel, gas station, café, store, post office and saloon. It took care of the needs of El Camino Sierra travelers for over 80 years.

Bill's son Tom took over management of Little Lake and the family continued on, until selling the historic property in 1952. The property changed owners a few more times over the next 38 years, closing in 1990 to conduct major renovations.

The hotel reopened in April of 1991 with great fanfare. A press release touted the new kitchen equipment, new carpeting, remodeled bathrooms and a state of the art septic system. Little Lake Hotel was poised to take care of yet another generation of El Camino Sierra travelers.

But on July 20, 1992, a fire broke out and despite the heroic efforts of several local volunteer and professional fire departments, the building suffered severe damage. Extensive building code requirements caused the current owners to decide not to attempt rebuilding. The hotel and all its services closed for good and the entire complex was leveled.

Today, highway 395 completely bypasses the site of Little Lake Hotel. All that remains are a few cement slabs, a little junk, and the sentimental memories of the tens of thousands of mountain bound travelers, who once stopped in to re-fresh and re-fuel, as they made their way toward their dreams…along El Camino Sierra.

CHAPTER FOUR

TERRIFYING TIOGA

The Eastern Sierra region has a history of roadways that have evoked an emotional response in the people that have known and used them. Many a traveler headed to the California goldfields was grateful and thankful for the presence of the Old Spanish Trail through southern Inyo County. That route led them to safety through some of the most desolate reaches known to exist. Bob Eichbaum's toll road from Darwin to Stovepipe Wells delivered many of the first tourists to the depths of Death Valley, who took in the overwhelming beauty of this mysterious and little known desert.

One roadway in particular generated a wide range of emotions from its users. To some, the thought of traveling on this rugged route created frightening nightmares. To others, its use meant traveling to an area where the possibility of striking it big was great. To all, the trip was as an experience that would likely not be soon forgotten.

Tioga Pass sits on the divide of the mighty Sierra Crest at an elevation of 9942 feet above sea level. The Tioga Pass road, also known now as California State Highway 120, leads from the stark and beautiful landscape of Mono Lake, up the yawning chasm of Lee Vining Canyon, under the shadow of 13,000 foot peaks, to the enchanted gardens of Yosemite National Park's Tuolumne Meadows.

The first route into this area was actually a few miles to the south of Tioga, known as Mono Pass. Native Americans made their way across these steep cliffs for hundreds of years to trade with their western neighbors. The U.S. Cavalry pursued Chief Tenaya and his band of Ahwahneechees across Mono Pass as they fled from their homes in Yosemite Valley. A few gold seekers even made the transit across this difficult route. For hundreds of years, trans-Sierra travel in this region was over the trail through Mono Pass.

In the 1880s, silver and gold were discovered on the slopes of Tioga Hill and above Lundy Canyon. The mines were located at elevations ranging from 9,000 feet to 10,500 feet. The extremely high elevation coupled with its remote location made operating the mines very difficult.

In 1882, two mules and a dozen men toiled eight weeks to drag, push and pull nearly 16,000 pounds of needed mining equipment to the new camp known as Bennettville.

The camp's organizers felt they had come upon a lode so rich, that 50,000 people would soon inhabit the site and a better road would be needed. In 1883, the mining company built a 56-mile road in from west in just 130 days. It became known as the Great Sierra Wagon Road. Like most mining camps, there were more dreams than rich ore. The new town and the road that served it were soon abandoned.

Eventually, the National Park Service took over the road (thanks to the generosity of its first director Stephen Mather) and the State of California extended the road east, from Tioga Pass down Lee Vining Canyon to the Mono Basin. It was one of the first highways built by the California Department of Highways and served adventurous Yosemite mountain visitors for the next several decades.

Figure 11-Travelers on the original Tioga Road could expect a slow trip.

Tioga Pass road received many improvements over the next few decades, but it mostly remained a narrow, winding, exposed and often potholed thoroughfare into the 1950s.

With the cessation of World War II, the American public went on the move. Visitation to the National Parks skyrocketed and the number of yearly travelers over the Tioga Pass Road soon numbered in the tens of thousands.

The increase in travelers brought a subsequent increase in highway incidents. The Lee Vining Canyon portion of the highway in particular, pushed several motorists to the edge of a nervous breakdown. The road was mostly one lane with turnouts, and often with no guardrails to protect motorists from the plummeting drop-offs. When cars met in the narrow sections, one driver would have to back up to an area that was wide enough to allow passing.

Figure 12- Until 1964, the Lee Vining Canyon section of the Tioga Road was one lane with pullouts Copyright 1962 California Department of Transportation, all rights reserved.

After a good deal of controversy, the National Park Service realigned and rebuilt the section of the road within Yosemite National Park. To the outrage of some including photographer Ansel Adams, road crews dynamited some of the magnificent granite domes to create the new and "improved road." The new modern Park section of the Tioga Pass Road opened in 1961.

No sooner was the Park's new section complete, than the State of California issued three contracts to rebuild the Lee Vining Canyon section of the highway. The design called for a wide two lane road with shoulders, guardrails where needed and several scenic turnouts. Terrifying Tioga would finally be tamed.

Once the improvements were made, travel along the Tioga Road exploded. Large RVs and buses could now easily make the trip into Yosemite from the east side.

Today, thousands of cars, buses and motor homes make the trip up Lee Vining Canyon and over Tioga Pass every day during the peak of summer. Perhaps nowhere else in the world is there scenic grandeur as easily accessible and enjoyed as from the Tioga Pass Road...departing from historic El Camino Sierra.

Figure 12A- The Tioga Road as it sweeps up Lee Vining Canyon from El Camino Sierra.

CHAPTER FIVE

MAMMOTH MOUNTAIN MAN

Today, visitors to the Eastern Sierra travel on the Highway 395 corridor year around. In fact, according to numbers put out from the Mammoth Lakes Bureau of Tourism, the number of winter visitors to this mountain town is nearly equal to those that come in the summer.

To be sure, due to its unique geographic location, Mammoth Mountain has been receiving the snowfall benefits of passing winter storms for tens of thousands of years. But it is thanks entirely to the efforts of one man, that the Eastern Sierra has grown winter recreation to the level of sophistication that has made it one of the world's premier destination ski resorts.

Dave McCoy spent his early years in southern California before moving to Washington State after the eighth grade. It was while living in Washington that Dave met some folks of Norwegian ancestry and learned about skiing. He made his first set of skis in his high school woodshop class.

Dave moved to Independence in the Eastern Sierra shortly after graduation from high school. It was here, while working at the restaurant, Jim's Place, that he met Rona. They soon married and have now enjoyed over seven decades of marital bliss.

Skiing was quickly becoming more popular in the U.S. Dave and a few friends constructed a simple rope tow that they could move to different locations along the Eastern Sierra. His primary location was just off Highway 395 on McGee Mountain, using parts from a Model A truck to operate a rope tow. There is a highway marker on Crowley Lake Drive (old Highway 395) placed there by the local E Clampus Vitus Chapter marking the nearby location of McCoy's McGee Mountain ski hill.

Figure 13- Skiing at McGee Mountain, one of Dave McCoy's first ski areas in the Eastern Sierra.

Dave got a job working as a hydrographer for the Los Angeles Department of Water and Power. His job was to travel on skis during the winter, measuring the snowpack at various backcountry locations throughout the Sierra Nevada. Dave quickly became familiar with what areas harbored the deepest snows. Dave and his friends soon began operating their portable ski tow on the snow-drenched north slope of Mammoth Mountain.

Shortly thereafter, the Forest Service posted a request for bids to develop a ski resort at Mammoth Mountain. Dave made a proposal, drawing up his business plan on a single sheet of paper. He drew three lines on it and called them chairlifts. The Forest Service was convinced, and gave Dave a permit to build the first ski lifts at Mammoth.

Dave was able to buy four surplus tracked military vehicles called Weasels to use at Mammoth Mountain. Some skiers would ride inside while others would hold on to ropes coming off the back as Dave would take them over the snow to the rope tows. Everyone would be singing and laughing as they were taken across the snow to the slopes. This was the beginning of Mammoth Mountain Ski Area.

Figure 14- Surplus military amphibious vehicles known as Weasels were used to get skiers to the rope tows at Mammoth Mountain in the '50s.

Dave worked out a deal with United Tramway Company to purchase and install a chair lift. Many of the holes for the towers were dug by hand by Dave and his friends. The beginning of Mammoth Mountain was truly a grass roots effort.

A ski lodge was built in 1953. According to Dave, people would come up and work for free because they loved Mammoth Mountain so much. He credits his employees and his customers for providing most of the good ideas to develop the resort.

Dave started a ski team at Mammoth Mountain in the 1960s and he soon had 14 Olympic racers on his team. In 1965, visitors were expressing their desire for access to the top of the mountain so they could ski the best slopes. A chairlift was not an option because the top was too exposed to the elements. Dave worked out a deal with a Swiss company for the mountain's first gondola, opening thousands of acres of new terrain for skiing.

In 1986, Dave bought nearby June Mountain and had plans to link it with Mammoth Mountain in the style of the grand European ski resorts. Alas, these plans were never able to materialize.

Mammoth Mountain Ski Area continued to grow and Dave kept reinvesting the profits to make improvements. Dave's interests turned to helping the town of Mammoth Lakes grow along with his ski area. He bought several parcels of land in town and practically gave them away to people that were willing to build hotels and restaurants.

In addition to the ski area, Dave launched the town's first water district, fire department and high school. In 1989, he founded the Mammoth Lakes Foundation, which helped fund Cerro Coso Community College. Over the years, the Foundation has provided over 650 scholarships to students who otherwise may not have been able to attend.

English poet William Blake once said, "Great things are done when men and mountains meet." Dave McCoy's life has melded well with his beloved Sierra Nevada Mountains, ever since his arrival in the 1930s. His positive influence on the lives of visitors and residents alike has become legendary. In a land of mammoth mountain landscapes, Dave McCoy has been a Mammoth Mountain of a man, making the turns…along El Camino Sierra.

Figure 15-A young Dave McCoy enjoying the slopes at an early Mammoth Mountain.

CHAPTER SIX

APPLE ORCHARDS
AND INTERNMENT

Most El Camino Sierra travelers are familiar with Manzanar National Historic Site, located six miles south of the town of Independence. The tragic and painful chapter of American history is retold by the National Park Service with world-class interpretive displays and exhibits.

The American government's internment of Japanese-Americans and American citizens shortly after the outbreak of World War II is a travesty of unimaginable proportion. The challenge that confronted the constitutional strength of America was unrivaled in our country's history.

Manzanar has not always had a history so full of turmoil and turpitude. Native Americans inhabited the Manzanar area for centuries prior to the arrival of European settlers in the mid-19th century. It is believed they enjoyed a peaceful and prosperous lifestyle along the mighty Sierra Nevada Mountains.

Because of good soil and the abundance of water from several nearby creeks, the first white settlers to arrive in the Owens Valley quickly took possession of these Native American lands and began growing several varieties of crops and farm products.

In 1909, the June 18th edition of the *Inyo Independent* newspaper published a story stating that George Chaffey from southern California had purchased several thousand acres of land around and to the south of Independence, with the purpose of wide scale development.

The newspaper's story explained how Chaffey planned to build small hydroelectric projects on nearby creeks, irrigate thousands of acres of land from local streams to grow crops, and build an electric powered railroad to haul the agricultural products to Los Angeles.

Figure 16-Native Americans have inhabited Manzanar for hundreds of years.

George Chaffey was the brother of William Chaffey. Together, they developed the planned utopian southern California communities of Ontario, Upland and Etiwanda. Apparently, Chaffey had intentions to build the same type of development in the Owens Valley.

The newspaper article mentions "A strip 80 feet in width will be used as a double boulevard extending from Independence to Lone Pine. Streets will be laid out parallel to this boulevard. In this manner, the rocky slopes at the foot of the mountains will be platted."

By 1912, Chaffey had adopted the name *Owens Valley Improvement Company* for his development. A letter to the Company's Board of Directors stated, "It is surprising to see the number of automobiles passing to and fro, and the frequent remarks made as to the prosperous looking condition of the

Owens Valley Improvement Company's Ranches." The letter also states "Apples have become a major crop being grown on the developed property."

Figure 17- Billboard advertising land for sale at George Chaffey's development.

Apples had become the dominant crop grown on Chaffey's development, though pears, peaches, watermelons, and numerous other crops were also grown. A town developed and was named Manzanar, gleaned from the Spanish word for apples, *manzana*. The town supported a school, church, store, several homes and a community hall.

The Los Angeles Aqueduct was completed in 1913. As Owens Valley water was sent to L.A., the thirsty and growing city quickly needed more. L.A. began buying up more water rights throughout the Owens Valley. Chaffey sold his land and water rights to the city in 1924, and several nearby farmers quickly followed suit. Some farmers leased their orchards back from the city while others moved away. The Los Angeles Department of Water & Power (LADWP) managed the Manzanar orchards until 1932 using Native American labor to care for the apple trees. The orchard and the remainder of the town were abandoned shortly thereafter.

At the end of the war when the Manzanar Internment Camp closed, the U.S. Government quickly took the camp down and removed the buildings. Several of the barracks and other structures were bought by Inyo County as well as nearby businesses and residents, who moved them to new locations throughout the County. A motel and two churches in Independence are built partially from buildings removed from the internment camp and nearby airfield.

Whether or not you have already visited Manzanar National Historic Site, consider stopping the next time you are in the area. Take in the exhibits and interpretive displays. Then spend some time out in the open spaces among the old fruit trees, and reflect upon all those that have come before, here in this land of many tales…told along El Camino Sierra.

Figure 18- Apples were grown commercially by the city of Los Angeles for a few years after they acquired the land and water rights at Manzanar.

CHAPTER SEVEN

WORTH SAVING

Travelers along El Camino Sierra are often surprised to see antlered animals much larger than the common Mule Deer, recurrently grazing in the fields throughout the Owens Valley. The Tule Elk is a magnificent creature that frequents the open country adjacent to Highway 395.

Their numbers have not always been so great. In 1874, there was just one breeding pair remaining in all of California. It is thanks to the efforts of one Owens Valley landowner who helped bring this regal symbol of the great American West back from the brink of extinction in the 1930s.

The Tule Elk are actually not native to Eastern California. Their ancestral domain was the marshes and grasslands of the great Central Valley and the grassy hills of the Coast Range. It is estimated their numbers were as high as 500,000 when the first European settlers arrived in California in the early 1700s.

As California grew, the elk population plummeted. Cattle and horses introduced by the Spaniards in the 18th century created competition for food. Wide scale hunting of the elk helped feed the thousands of '49er gold-miners and further led to their decline. By the 1870s, it was thought the Tule Elk had become extinct, when a state game warden discovered a single breeding pair on a cattle ranch near Tulare.

The two remaining elk were quickly placed under protection and an aggressive recovery effort was put in place. The population at first resurged, but then habitat loss and poaching took their toll. The state's population again dwindled to just 28 Tule Elk by 1895.

State fish and wildlife agents once again stepped in to aggressively manage the remaining elk. During the next several years, no fewer than 21 attempts were made to transplant elk to different locales throughout the state.

Sequoia and Yosemite National Parks, among other places, were thought to be ideal locations for the elk.

But each of the relocation efforts failed to produce positive results. In 1933, rangers in Yosemite were looking for a place to move the herd of 27 Tule Elk from the Park. Conditions were just too cold for the elk, and the Park Service kept them hemmed in on a 28-acre piece of Park land.

Owens Valley businessman and conservationist Walter Dow came to the rescue. He initiated and financed the transplanting of the 27 elk to the ranch he owned in the Owens Valley. The following year, Dow arranged to bring an additional 28 elk from a reserve the state had established near Tupman, California.

Figure 19-Elk transported in crates being unloaded at Walter Dow's ranch in the Owens Valley.

Though not native to the Owens Valley, the elk thrived at their new home. Dow fed the elk on his property, but keeping the 600-pound wapiti on only his ranch proved impossible. The growing herd made their way to the alfalfa fields of other ranchers and to nearby lands owned by the Los Angeles Department of Water and Power (LADWP).

By the early 1960s, the herd had grown to an estimated 300. Fences and valuable crops were being destroyed. Ranchers began to complain there were "too many" elk in the Owens Valley. Hunting of the elk was approved by the state to cull their numbers.

Figure 20-Dow feeding the Tule Elk at their new home in the Owens Valley.

Fearful the Tule Elk would once again face the possibility of extinction, Dow formed the Committee for the Preservation of Tule Elk. The committee lobbied the City of Los Angeles to set aside 240 square miles of their Inyo County land as a preserve for the elk, and for the State to reconsider their decision to allow elk hunting.

Politics and legal wrangling held play on the "elk issue" for the next ten years. In 1971, California passed legislation (the Behr bill) requiring that the elk not be hunted until their numbers statewide surpassed 2,000 head or until it could be determined that suitable elk habitat no longer existed in the state, and mandated the California Department of Resources to reintroduce the elk into former habitats wherever possible.

By 1976, the U.S. House and Senate weighed in, passed a resolution that 2,000 was the correct number of Tule Elk, and directed U.S. agencies to make federal land available for the elk's preservation. An interagency task force with members from state and federal agencies was set up to select sites for the reintroduction of elk. Elk were introduced in eight different California locations. Fish and Wildlife managers put the total state population today at about 4,200 in 22 different herds.

Rarely does one person have such a significant impact as saving an entire species from extinction. Walter Dow's initiative to take matters into his own hands kept the world from losing yet another member of its animal kingdom. But Dow's good deeds didn't stop with his involvement with the elk.

By the early 1920s Hollywood had discovered the abundance of natural settings in the Lone Pine area that were perfect for making movies and Dow foresaw the benefits the movie industry could bring to the town. Movie companies would need lodging while filming on location and Dow built Lone Pine's historic Dow Hotel. Over the years, the Dow Hotel, as well as the Dow Villa Motel built by Joe and Verna Bonham in the early 1960s, have played host to thousands of Hollywood producers, directors and movie stars.

As Inyo County grew, Dow felt the Inyo County seat of Independence should have lodging worthy of the important people that would come to do business with the county. In 1927, Dow opened the luxury Winnedumah Hotel in Independence, catering to the needs of the well-heeled traveler.

Dow and his wife Maude also felt it was vitally important for small communities such as Inyo County, to do all they could to preserve their history. The Eastern California Museum in Independence was built thanks largely to the generosity of the Dows.

Walter and Maude Dow, truly citizens extraordinaire who helped make life that much better...along El Camino Sierra.

Figure 21-Owens Valley businessman and philanthropist Walter Dow.

CHAPTER EIGHT

SOARING TO NEW HEIGHTS

Promotion and advertising are certainly not ideas that just came about in the past few decades. People have been promoting their products, ideas and events since the first Homo sapiens stood upright.

The idea of a grand Sierra Highway to be known as El Camino Sierra was a good one to be sure. But securing the necessary funding from the state highway commission would be a challenge. When the first highway bonds were passed in 1910, Inyo and Mono Counties combined had only 9,000 of the state's 2.4 million residents. A lot of interest in the area would have to be generated if there was any hope in getting state road money for their rural area.

The Inyo Good Roads Club had several skilled marketers among its officers, not the least of which was W. Gillette Scott. He was first to coin the name El Camino Sierra, as well as promote travel over a grand circuit route to be known as the Pasear.

In 1914, Scott devised yet another means to get Sacramento politicians and department heads to take notice of the other side of California. Those daring young men (and women) in their flying machines were drawing the public's attention everywhere they went. The barnstorming adventures of these aviators could be read about in the newspapers almost daily.

Scott and the Inyo Good Roads Club came up with an idea they called "Eastern Sierra Aviation Days." The highlight of the event would be for an aviator to fly their plane over the top of Mt. Whitney, the highest mountain in the 48 states...an attention grabber to be sure.

The Inyo Good Roads Club raised prize money from local businesses to be awarded to the successful aviator. $1,000 to the pilot who would attempt it and $2,000 if the flight were successful.

Silas Christofferson was only 24 years old when the Inyo Good Roads Club contacted him. Christofferson already had an impressive resume of aeronautical stunts including flying a plane off a hotel rooftop in Portland, Oregon. His youthfulness and indomitable spirit made him the perfect candidate for the stunt and he enthusiastically accepted the challenge.

Figure 22-Silas Christofferson with his wife Emma.

The design work and construction of Christofferson's plane was considered state of the art for the time. Christofferson contracted with the Curtiss aeroplane company of New York to build him a special plane at the pricey cost of $7,000. Once completed, the plane was shipped to Bishop in pieces, and reassembled upon arrival.

Christofferson kicked off the festivities with exhibitions flights at Bishop which coincided with the celebration of the upcoming event. Eastern Sierra Aviation Days were said to have been the largest gathering of people in the Owens Valley up to that time.

The next few days saw Christofferson test his aircraft in the sometimes-difficult weather of the Owens Valley. A few record setting attempts were made only to be aborted due to powerful winds. A violent and sudden downdraft nearly caused the plane and pilot to crash during one of his runs.

Finally, early on Thursday morning June 25th, Christofferson took off from Lone Pine to attempt the record setting flight. He made it to 13,400 but had to call it off when high winds once again kept him away from the mountain's summit.

Returning to Lone Pine, he replaced the propeller with one he felt would work better, and removed the movie camera to save weight. He took off again at 8:30 a.m. for a second attempt. Photographer Bertie Forbes had hoped to get pictures of the historic event from Mt. Whitney' summit, but on the way up, his mule slipped and the photography equipment shattered in the fall.

Figure 23-Christofferson and his crew preparing the plane for its historic flight.

Christofferson held the plane steady as he continued to gain altitude heading his aircraft towards Mt. Whitney. Observers from the valley below strained to catch a glimpse through telescopes and binoculars. Finally, the plane circled the top of the summit at an elevation of 15,728 feet. The American altitude record had been attained!

A quick descent was made back to the landing field where throngs of well-wishers greeted Christofferson and carried him on their shoulders to his waiting wife Emma.

W. Gillette Scott and the Inyo Good Roads club wasted no time in getting the word out that a new record had been set in the land of El Camino Sierra. A telegram was sent to the vice president of the Western Highway Association; "Inyo Good Roads Club this morning 9:00 a.m., achieved national prominence by sending Silas Christofferson in a tractor biplane over Mt. Whitney to a height of 15,728 feet, more than 1,226 feet above the summit, breaking all American records for altitude."

Unfortunately, Christofferson died in a plane crash while testing a new design just two years later. It's uncertain if Christofferson's record setting flight directly affected any decisions regarding funding for highways in the Eastern Sierra. But it is certain that a man of great courage and fortitude, helped bring the focus of the world to the land of great mountains and enormous landscapes...located sublimely along El Camino Sierra.

Figure 23A-The seal commemorating Christofferson's historic flight.

CHAPTER NINE

LONE PINE ASHRAM

Located high on the south slope above Tuttle Creek lies one of the most interesting architectural oddities found in the Eastern Sierra. The Lone Pine Ashram is a beautiful stone structure made of native Sierra granite and nestled among a forest of stately Piñon Pines. How the structure got there is another one of the hundreds of interesting tales to be found along El Camino Sierra.

Franklin Merrell-Wolff was born in Pasadena, California in 1887. The eldest of three children, Franklin was raised in a household whose Methodist minister father was also a pioneer in California's citrus industry. Wolff was home-schooled by his mother until the age of nine.

According to Wolff's biography, when he reached his teenage years, he began to question some of his father's theological doctrine. He questioned the belief in having unwavering faith to a higher deity and made a decision to leave traditional Christian religion.

Wolff's orientation to what he referred to as "sound thinking" and his interest in truth led him to the study of mathematics. He entered Stanford University in 1907, where he majored in pure mathematics, and minored in psychology and philosophy. After graduation, he enrolled in a master's program at Harvard where he submerged himself in philosophy classes.

Wolf wasn't committed to staying in academia. He found himself wondering if the antinomies of the subject-object consciousness could be found. Wolff joined a philosophical colony in Carmel, California where he soon met his wife Sherifa.

For the next several years, Wolff and Sherifa followed several different teachers of Theosophy (the nature of divinity and the origin and purpose of the universe). In 1928, Wolf and Sherifa founded the Assembly of Man, an educational center that adopted a generally theosophical orientation.

Figure 24-Franklin Wolff and his wife Sherifa.

The couple had been told by an Indian philosopher that the spiritual center of a country was close to its highest point of elevation. Wolff and Sherifa chose to head to Hunter's Camp (now known as Whitney Portal) to work on various writing projects. They set up their camp near a waterfall and spent the next two months writing and contemplating in the shadow of Mt. Whitney.

The couple decided to start a summer school near the area where they had camped. Wolff inquired of the U.S. Forest Service about a special use permit for the school and was informed that in order to receive authorization for such an operation in the High Sierra Primitive Area (as it was known at the time), the Assembly would need to erect some sort of permanent structure. Moreover, he was told that building permits for the Hunter's Camp area were not available.

Wolff explored the next canyon south of Hunter's Camp for a suitable site for their summer school. He found a spot high in a beautiful Piñon Pine forest surrounded by two branches of Tuttle Creek. The founders of the Assembly of Man decided the remote and quiet wilderness of Tuttle Creek Canyon would provide the ideal atmosphere for their school.

Wolff received permission from the Forest Service to operate a summer school on Tuttle Creek in 1929, and work began on preparing a site for a structure the very next year. Wolff used dynamite to blast a flat area and as rock began piling up, he got the idea to use it in the construction of the building. The structure was laid out roughly along the four cardinal points of the compass, and built in the shape of a balanced cross to symbolize the principle of equilibrium.

Figure 25-The Tuttle Creek Ashram is accessible by a fairly short hike.

Lumber and cement were initially brought to the site by burros from Olivas Ranch, which was located on the north side of the canyon. Wolff later cleared an access road on the south side of the canyon, which could accommodate a tractor pulling a flatbed trailer. Wolff and his students would work on the Ashram the next twenty summers, spending their days engaged in hard labor and their evenings with music and study around a campfire. The group also held formal services at the site, with Wolff and Sherifa officiating.

A large altar was constructed on the floor of the structure using randomly patterned granite stones set in mortar. The altar was topped by a smooth covering of mortar, which was later inscribed upon by an unknown visitor in the 1960s.

In 1951, with the structure still not complete, Wolff stopped work because Sherifa was no longer able to make the trip to the building site due to an illness. Wolff lost interest in its completion and the building was left with no windows or doors. The ashram soon began to fall into disrepair.

The stone structure has been referred to by a number of different names over the years: Summer Camp, Rama Sangha School and the Ajna Ashrama to name just a few. Today members of the Franklin Merrell-Wolff Fellowship refer to it simply as "The Ashram." Lone Pine residents often refer to it as "The Monastery" and one can find it called "The Stone House" in hiking guides. It is known to the U.S. Forest Service as the "Tuttle Creek Ashram."

When Congress passed the Wilderness Act in 1964, it was thought the ashram might be demolished when the area was included inside the John Muir Wilderness. Since the school had not been used for over ten years, the Forest Service was able to declare Wolff's permit void due to abandonment. It was reported the Forest Service considered dynamiting the structure into rubble.

No demolition occurred. The Forest Service re-evaluated it for its historical importance and concluded that the structure was indeed significant. The California State Historic Preservation Office concurred. The ashram has since been nominated for recognition in the National Register of Historic Places. Today, the Ashram is in surprisingly good shape and enjoys a peaceful existence in the shadows of Mt. Whitney. The road to the trailhead is usually passable for passenger cars. A one and three quarter mile roundtrip hike leads to the ashram. As with all historical structures, please be respectful and leave the site even nicer than you find it if you visit, so others may enjoy this little piece of interesting history that can be found…not far from El Camino Sierra.

CHAPTER TEN

SKYWAY TO THE MOUNTAINS

Most Eastern Sierra residents and visitors are familiar with the scenic drive to Onion Valley from the town of Independence. The road is a masterpiece of engineering, climbing 5,200 feet in just thirteen miles, with a grade rarely exceeding ten percent.

The road ends in a small mountain valley, with jaw dropping mountain scenery, three waterfalls, a delightful U.S. Forest Service campground, a pack station, two trailheads and a very large parking area. The highly popular trail over Kearsarge Pass starts here and climbs 2,500 feet, providing fairly easy access to some of the best of Kings Canyon National Park's phenomenal backcountry. The area is named *Onion Valley* for the wild onion that can be found here in this peaceful and mostly quiet setting.

Looking back to 1959 when this modern roadway was being built tells us much about highway construction. According to an article in the *L.A. Times* from that year, the City of Los Angeles and Inyo County worked together to build a new and improved roadway to Onion Valley. There was great excitement in Inyo, and for good reason. There were plans at that time, to not only complete the paved road to Onion Valley, but to keep right on going up and over the 11,709 feet Kearsarge Pass and down Bubbs Creek to Cedar Grove in Kings Canyon National Park.

"Work has been in progress for several seasons, municipal and county forces forging ahead. Excellent progress has been made." said the *Times* story. The article goes on to say that as of that date, Inyo County had spent the whopping sum of $25,000, the City of Los Angeles $16,000 and that the U.S. Forest Service had contributed a carload of powder, three-fourths of which would be left over for use on the planned Horseshoe Meadows Road.

Figure 26-Inyo county and the LADWP worked together to build the new modern roadway to Onion Valley in the late '50s and early '60s.

The *Times* article mentions that Los Angeles has "dual interests" in the road being built. First, it will be another place of recreation the people of Los Angeles can vacation to, and also "by rearing small dams at the lakes in the Onion Valley area, the flood waters now going to waste down the main creek, can be controlled and a much more extensive acreage about Independence put under cultivation."

The plans called for Los Angeles to help build the road past Onion Valley to the vicinity of Gilbert, Flower and Matlock lakes (about 2 ½ to 3 miles by foot trail). Each lake would have a small dam placed at its outlet to raise its storage capacity. From Flower Lake, Inyo County was responsible to build the road the final two-plus miles to Kearsarge Pass.

It was estimated this part of the road to the pass would take several "seasons" to build but once completed the story gushes, "The road will tap matchless recreational area in which the whole nation may turn, as it becomes more and more the nation's playground. If you would think of eternity, look upon the High Sierra."

At the time, the area just west of Kearsarge Pass was not yet part of Kings Canyon National Park (this part wasn't added until 1965). To add to the excitement, LADWP commissioner William Whitsett and retired Inyo County Supervisor George Naylor proposed to the California State Parks Commission, that the high mountain area west of Kearsarge Pass should be turned into a California State Park.

Whitsett is quoted, "The area is a combination of everything stupendous, fascinating and spectacular possessed by all our national playgrounds with the exception of the Yellowstone geysers and is ideal in every respect. Mr. Naylor, was the first ranger there, thirty years ago, long before the national forests were organized, and knows every feature of it and is one of its strongest proponents."

Naylor is also quoted in the article "A drive such as this, passing through two parks, through Kings River Canyon on to Kearsarge Pass and its glorious overlook upon a lower realm could not be equaled elsewhere on the globe."

Figure 27-Kearsarge Pass trail. The proposed trans-Sierra route would have passed over the Sierra crest here on its way to Cedar Grove in Kings Canyon.

The columnist goes on "That most terse description ever applied to the Grand Canyon 'It's so damned big that you can't lie about it' fits the grandeur of this ensemble with equal appropriateness. Last year, Mr. Whitsett went to the Alps and saw them as virtual dwarfs in contrast with the heaven-puncturing domain at our own doorsteps."

If building this grand road wouldn't be enough, the columnist suggests the possibility of creating artificial waterfalls along the proposed road for people to enjoy. It is pointed out that "comparatively little difficulty or cost would be incurred by simply diverting certain streams into manmade drops of perhaps 2,000 feet, and though nature has been lavish with her creations, the added falls would improve upon them."

The story concludes, "Here lies an idle asset of the Owens and San Joaquin Valleys and of Los Angeles and all of southern California that should be developed because it would provide us forever a pleasure ground without peer, and add immeasurable to the joy, health, wealth and fame of the community."

As we know today, the new and improved Onion Valley Road was only completed as far as Onion Valley. One can still get to Kearsarge Pass, but only on foot or horseback. In 1964, the John Muir Wilderness was created and any plans to extend the road past Onion Valley were dashed.

In 1965, Kings Canyon National Park was expanded and the vast mountain wilderness just west of Kearsarge Pass gained federal protection, removing any prospect of it becoming a State Park. Everything in life is relative. This was obviously a time where many people thought building roads most anywhere was a great idea and that humans "improving" the landscape made perfect sense. Times change along El Camino Sierra…and so do we.

CHAPTER ELEVEN

IRREPRESSIBLE CHARLES BROWN

Eastern California has long been a place of famous landmarks: Mt. Whitney, the highest peak in the contiguous United States; Death Valley, the lowest place in the Western hemisphere and the Bristlecone Pine Trees, the oldest living things on earth. And though not large in population, El Camino Sierra country can certainly boast its share of landmark people as well.

A case could be made for one person in the area's rich history being among the most influential and powerful lawmakers the great state of California has ever seen: Charles Brown.

Born in Georgia in 1883, Brown arrived by train in Tehachapi, California in 1908. It was a blistering hot summer day and when a stranger offered Brown some mulligan stew, Brown asked the man if he had any water. The man dipped a can into a nearby stagnant pond and strained it through his grimy shirt. Brown ignored the squirming pollywogs stranded in the cloth and gratefully drank the liquid.

Talk in Tehachapi's hobo camp was about the mining boom happening at Greenwater, on the brink of Death Valley. Charlie quickly made his way to Greenwater and found work at the mine.

A natural leader, Brown was soon approached by townsfolk to take on the job of Deputy Sheriff in the lawless mining camp. Brown accepted and thus Charles Brown's long career in public service had begun.

Brown tackled his new position in law enforcement with gusto. He soon gained the respect of most of the town for his diligence to do right and bring about justice. Brown arrested one particularly obnoxious miner who had been threatening townsfolk with a gun. Having no cell to hold him in until the Sheriff from Independence could arrive to take him to jail; Brown housed the prisoner at his own tent and took away his pants and shoes to discourage an escape. Brown awoke the next morning to find the prisoner had vanished, along with Brown's only pair of shoes! Brown was determined to find him and in his stocking feet, soon tracked down the errant prisoner.

Brown befriended a prominent Greenwater businessman named R.J. "Dad" Fairbanks. He not only admired Fairbank's business acumen, but also noticed that Fairbanks had a beautiful daughter named Stella.

The Greenwater boom busted quickly into one of the greatest investment frauds California has ever known and the town soon emptied. Now unemployed Brown went to work for Dad Fairbanks, partly for the income and mostly so he could stay close to court Stella.

Dad Fairbanks, with the help and hard work of Brown, started the town of Shoshone, first as a station for the Borax Company's railroad, and later as a stopover for tourists driving to Death Valley. Fairbanks moved on to create the town of Baker on the L.A. to Las Vegas highway, and left Brown to watch over Shoshone.

Brown eventually won the heart and hand of Stella in marriage. The Browns raised their four children in Shoshone as their successful businesses continued to grow.

Figure 28-Charles & Stella Brown.

The Browns became the patriarch family of Shoshone. Brown became keenly aware of the needs of the small community and helped establish the first school in the area that educated not only the Brown's children, but also those of local Native American families.

Tired of seeing what he felt was a tendency for Inyo County government officials to ignore this far off and remote area of the county in funding as well as needs, Brown decided to run for County Supervisor in 1924. There had never been a County Supervisor from eastern Inyo County. With less than 40 voters in this area, his friends told him he "had about as much chance as a wax mouse racing an asbestos cat through hell." Brown replied, "I'll let them know someone lives over here anyway."

Brown knocked on the door of most every house in his district including remote mining camps, and the town of Lone Pine, 160 miles distant. When the votes were counted, Brown was the new county supervisor for the southern (and eastern) area of Inyo County.

Charles Brown became an ardent advocate for all of rural Inyo County. The terrible condition of the area's roads forced Brown to often take a roundabout route to get to the monthly supervisor's meetings in Independence. Brown's trip started by taking the railroad from Shoshone south to Baker, the Union Pacific Railroad from Baker all the way into downtown Los Angeles, and from there, the L.A. Aqueduct railroad (Southern Pacific) up to the Owens Valley. A three-day trip for what now takes about three hours.

The Borax Company was developing tourism in Death Valley and the new and nearby Arrowhead Highway (now I-15) would soon be bringing thousands of travelers through the upper Mojave. Brown knew if he could get good roads through this area, travelers would come and everyone would benefit. Brown made many trips to see the San Bernardino County supervisors to sell the idea of paving their county highway from Baker north to the Inyo County line, where he promised them he would get Inyo County to pave the road the remainder of the distance into Death Valley. They did and he did. Tourists could now visit the mysterious Death Valley via the comforts of a modern paved road.

Brown served tirelessly as county supervisor for 14 years. In 1938, Brown ran for the position of State Senator for all of Inyo, Mono and Alpine counties and won handily. He served his constituents in Eastern California faithfully for 25 years and become one of the most powerful and effective legislators in Sacramento. His influence became legendary as fellow legislators had to commonly "first run things by Charlie" before introducing their own legislation in the state legislature.

His major interests were rural roads, mining, and fish and game. He was instrumental in acquiring state funds to help build and maintain the Visitor

Center in Death Valley. His legacy lives on throughout Eastern California, which has one of the finest networks of state and county roads to be found in such a remote and rural area.

Brown passed away in 1963 and is buried with his wife Stella in their beloved town of Shoshone. All of Eastern California has greatly benefited from the hard work and dedication of public philanthropist Charles Brown. His legacy also lives on through his grandchildren Susan Sorrels and Brian Brown who both play a large role in the Southeast Inyo County Community.

Figure 29-Charles Brown (third from right) and party atop Dantes View in Death Valley.

CHAPTER TWELVE

A SHOWPLACE FOR ALL TIME

Some things are well deserving of the term "institution." The history behind them and their stature in the community they serve, places them in this esteemed regard. One such place worthy of this title is located just a few miles outside the town of Independence.

The Mt. Whitney Fish Hatchery has been an important landmark along El Camino Sierra since its completion in 1917. On land purchased and donated by the citizens of Independence, the California State Fish and Game Commission constructed what was at the time the largest and best-equipped fish hatchery in the state. "Design a building that would match the mountains, would last forever and would be a showplace for all time," instructed Fish and Game Commissioner M.J. Connell, and his instructions were followed to the letter.

The magnificent structure was built in Tudor Revival style out of 3,200 tons of granite rock collected within a quarter mile radius of the site. The massive stone walls are two to three feet thick and complimented beautifully by the red Spanish tile roof.

When first opened, it was able to produce over two million fish fry per year. Golden Trout eggs were collected from the Rae Lakes area of what is now Kings Canyon National Park. They were transported to the Hatchery in milk cans lashed to the backs of mules, which made their way carefully over the High Sierra mountain passes to bring the prized eggs to the Hatchery.

In 1919, the state began collecting Golden Trout eggs from the Cottonwood Lakes near Horseshoe Meadows. Since that time, this area has served as the only source of eggs for the California State Fish. This rare species is now raised at the Owens Valley's Black Rock Fish Hatchery.

Figures 30-(above) & 31-(below)-Fish fry were often transported in milk cans lashed to mules and packed over steep mountain passes.

Over the years, the Mt. Whitney Fish Hatchery became much more than just a location to raise trout fry. The beautiful building and grounds became a centerpiece for southern Inyo and the people of Independence. Countless high school graduations have been held there. The hatchery grounds have served as the location for hundreds of weddings, family reunions and community events. The community came to think of the Hatchery as their own.

State budget cuts followed by a wild land fire in 2007 and a devastating flash flood and mudflow in 2008 brought the great Hatchery to its knees. The mudflow destroyed the Hatchery's infrastructure and its ability to raise the fish fry and the State decided to close the historic site.

But typical of many small communities, the good folks of Independence and southern Inyo County rallied together. They couldn't just let the great building and all it represented, fade away into obscurity or be on the leeward side of a wrecking ball. The non-profit Friends of the Mt. Whitney Fish Hatchery (FMWFH) was created with the purpose of managing the building and its grounds. Though fish would no longer be raised there, FMWFH would operate a small demonstration hatchery with an interpretive exhibit. FMWFH would keep the Hatchery and its grounds open for visitors and locals to enjoy.

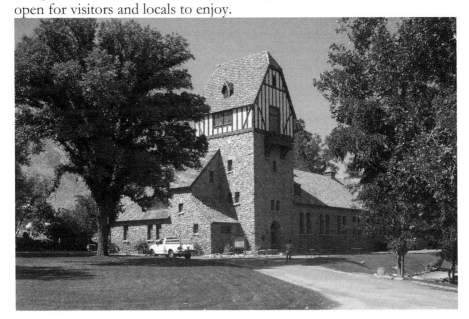

Figure 32-The Mt Whitney Fish Hatchery is built with blocks of granite up to three feet thick.

Taking on such an undertaking is not an easy or inexpensive task. The FMWFH is an all-volunteer organization and relies heavily on the thousands of hours of hard work performed by its dozens of supporters, as it has become one of the most visited tourist spots in southern Inyo County.

Small town ethos goes a long way in preserving and keeping alive an area's history, heritage and tradition. Without the commitment of its dedicated supporters, the Mt. Whitney Fish Hatchery may not still be here for all of us to enjoy.

The Mt. Whitney Fish Hatchery is located about three miles north of the town of Independence just off El Camino Sierra. Turn west on signed Fish Hatchery Rd (2.3 miles north of Independence) and follow it just over a mile to the Hatchery on the right.

Figure 32A-The Hatchery was built on land donated by residents of the town of Independence.

CHAPTER THIRTEEN

ABOVE ALL OTHERS

If the Eastern Sierra had no attractions other than Mt. Whitney itself, people would still flock to the area to see and experience the great mountain in numbers rivaling the population of a small state. There is a special magic about Mt. Whitney that has drawn people to it for 150 years. Whether gazing at the majestic peak from along El Camino Sierra, negotiating the twists and turns of Whitney Portal Road, or making the long climb to its summit-the highest spot in the contiguous United States…the faithful seem to hear as John Muir once did, "The mountains are calling…and I must go."

At 14,505 feet, Mt. Whitney is the highest peak in the lower 48 states. In 1864 while working in the Eastern Sierra, members of the California Geological Survey named the peak after their boss Josiah Whitney, the State Geologist of California at that time.

Figure 33-Mt. Whitney viewed from the Alabama Hills.

Originally, this peak was referred to by local Paiute and Shoshone as "Too-man-i-goo-yah," which translates to "guardian spirit." Native Americans have inhabited the Owens Valley and Eastern Sierra for thousands of years and their ancestors were undoubtedly the first human beings to stand upon its summit.

During the 1864 California Survey, geologist Clarence King attempted to climb Whitney from its west side, but was stopped just short of its summit. King returned in 1871 to attempt another climb to what he believed to be Mt. Whitney, but having taken a different approach, he actually summited nearby Mt. Langley.

Learning he had a made a mistake, King struck out in September of 1873, to continue his quest to be the first non-Native American to reach its summit, but he was too late. In August of that year, three men from Lone Pine and Independence, Charles Begole, A.H. Johnson and John Lucas, had already made the first recorded ascent to its summit. They chose to name the mountain "Fishermans Peak."

Residents of the Owens Valley liked the name "Fishermans Peak." King challenged the name and Lone Pine folks countered with the name "Dome of Inyo." A bill was introduced in the California State Legislature making Fishermans Peak the official name, but the governor vetoed the bill. Finally, after ten years of wrangling, the name Mt. Whitney was officially recognized by both the state and federal governments.

Hiking alone from Independence in 1873, John Muir became the next person recorded to have made it to Whitney's summit. Muir approached the peak via its north face, by what now is called "the Mountaineer's Route."

For the next 20 years, the trip to the top was a dangerous one. A narrow trail was beaten out by boots but the upper part was dangerous for stock and pack animals. Realizing the huge tourism potential of having the nation's tallest peak in its front yard, the citizens of Lone Pine raised enough money to build a good trail for tourists to travel to Whitney's summit in 1904.

Lone Pine local Gustave Marsh was hired to design and build a trail to the top, manageable by both humans and stock animals. The trail was completed and its opening celebrated on July 22, 1904. Firewood was hauled to the summit by mules and a huge bonfire was set. The fire, easily seen from Lone Pine, was meant to signal the townsfolk that the trail was completed.

An employee from the U.S. Department of Fish and Wildlife was struck and killed by lightning on Whitney's summit just four days after the trail was completed. Because scientists would be using the summit of Mt. Whitney for conducting high altitude tests, the Smithsonian Institute and the Lick Observatory came up with funds to build a stone hut on its summit to protect the workers from the elements. Marsh was once again contracted to do the work. The 11 x 30-foot rock building still stands solidly at the summit, though high altitude testing is no longer conducted. The structure is listed on the U.S. National Register of Historic Places.

Figure 34-The "Smithsonian Institution Shelter" on the summit of Mt. Whitney was built by Lone Pine resident Gustave Marsh.

Marsh's trail started down at Lone Pine Campground since there was no road to Whitney Portal at that time. As part of Franklin Roosevelt's New Deal, the Civilian Conservation Corps (CCC) was brought in to construct a new "auto road" in 1936 to be called the Whitney Portal Road. The road was another of those marvels of engineering that seems to be almost commonplace in the Eastern Sierra. The CCC Lone Pine Camp worked on dozens of other Inyo National Forest and Eastern California projects.

With increasing demands from visitors now able to drive further up the mountain, the Mt. Whitney Pack Trains built a store and corrals at Whitney

Figure 35-Whitney Portal Road construction in 1933 by the CCC.

Portal. In 1938, the Whitney Trail was rebuilt by the Forest Service with Chrysler and Cook's Mt. Whitney Pack Trains of Lone Pine hauling up all of the supplies for the trail crew. A back-country camp operated for a short period along the trail at Outpost Camp, providing comfortable beds and meals for travelers to Mt. Whitney.

In the 1940s, the Forest Service wanted to rebuild and realign some of the steeper parts of the trail. Rock drills would be required for some of the work. A much needed 10,000-pound air compressor was taken apart and its pieces hauled eight miles up to the jobsite by mule-power, where it was reassembled. The largest single part was a crankshaft weighing 344 pounds!

Hollywood movie-studios discovered the beautiful scenery at Whitney Portal would work perfectly for some of their films. The character of Mad Dog Earl, played by Humphrey Bogart in the movie *High Sierra*, met his fate at the hands of the law on the slopes above the Whitney Portal store. This is where they filmed the last scene, where Bogart uttered his famous final line, "That's what you think coppers" before being brought down by police sharpshooters. Lucille Ball and Desi Arnaz' character's fateful trip over the steep Sierra Mountain pass in the movie *The Long, Long Trailer* was skillfully filmed on the Whitney Portal Road.

Figure 36-Some scenes from Desi Arnaz and Lucille Ball's Long, Long Trailer were filmed on the Whitney Portal Rd. in 1953.

In the 1960s and '70s, as hiking and backpacking became more and more popular, so did attempts to get to the summit of Mt. Whitney. On busy summer weekends, 300 people would often make it to the summit. On one Labor Day Saturday, 1,500 hikers arrived at the top. The numbers were overwhelming and caused the Forest Service to enlist the help of a helicopter to remove the garbage left behind by the mass of humanity.

In 1971, Inyo National Forest implemented a wilderness permit system, which required hikers to state the number in party, point of entry, exit location, days of use etc. This information was analyzed and studied, and a quota permit system was developed.

In an effort to minimize the human impact on this most popular of hiking destinations, the Forest Service implemented a variety of regulations.

Currently, the number of people allowed to enter from the Whitney Portal trailhead is limited to 160 per day and are selected by a lottery. Camping along the trail is restricted to specific locations and hikers are required to carry out their solid human waste as well as their garbage.

Mt. Whitney and Whitney Portal remain some of the most popular destinations in the Eastern Sierra. For nearly 150 years, whether it be lunch at the Portal Cafe or a climb to its lofty summit, visitors and locals alike make their personal pilgrimage to an often times life moving experience at this most magical of locations...found along El Camino Sierra.

Figure 37-Some of the first tourists to take advantage of the "new" Whitney Portal Road.

CHAPTER FOURTEEN

BRINGING LIFE TO THE DESERT

Using irrigation to grow crops in the Eastern Sierra has been a practice long before white settlers arrived. Evidence suggests that Native Americans had dug ditches by hand to divert streams to areas suitable to grow food, enabling them to feed their families for hundreds of years.

Once settlers did arrive, they also constructed miles of irrigation ditches and soon had transformed tens of thousands of acres of arid Owens Valley into productive agricultural lands.

Early on, most of the interest in agriculture was focused to the north, around Bishop and Round Valley. Though the southern part of the Owens Valley near Independence and Lone Pine was not as developed, there was one south county area that was for a time, the focus of a huge and ambitious farming project.

In January of 1900, an article appeared in *The American Friend*, a publication of the Quaker Church, announcing the formation of the William Penn Colonial Association. The article stated that the object of the Association was "to promote a colony embodying features that were attractive to "Friends" throughout the United States."

The article goes on to say that a committee of "Friends" from the Whittier area of southern California recently had traveled to the Owens Valley of California to examine 14,000 acres of land. The committee was researching the conditions that would affect its desirability as a place to locate such a colony. The committee declared, "That the soil is fertile and productive is demonstrated at Lone Pine Station which adjoins this land, where in similar soils, crops are grown to perfection."

A group from the Whittier area of southern California was making plans to develop thousands of acres of the Owens Valley into an agricultural super farm. The committee saw the abundant water in the streams from the Sierra Nevada (this was pre L.A. diversions) and concluded the use of irrigation would be quite feasible.

The McIver Canal had already been in existence in the southeast part of Owens Valley since the 1880s. In fact, by 1900, over 40 miles of irrigation canals existed in this area.

By 1902, The William Penn Colonial Association had exercised its purchase option on 13,000 acres of land and began offering 40 acres parcels for sale at $25 per acre.

Figure 38-Prospectus pamphlet for the William Penn Colonial Association's planned development in southern Inyo County.

At first the Colony promoted sugar beets and alfalfa as the crops that would be most productive. The Association's self-published prospectus pamphlet also mentioned that alfalfa would draw honey bees, enabling the farmers to have yet another agricultural commodity to harvest.

The Southern Pacific Railroad had announced plans to run a rail line through the area, further increasing the enthusiasm of the developers. The train would be able to haul the Colony's farm products to distant markets.

A town was established by the Colony and given the name Owenyo, a portmanteau of Owens and Inyo. A post office was located at Owenyo in March of 1902, and due to the "roaming" nature of the Colony and its town, it moved at least twice in the next three years.

Figure 39-The town of Owenyo became an important railroad community in the Owens Valley after the Colony sold its land.

The prospectus pamphlet touted the availability of cheap water, abundance of wildlife, proximity to nearby profitable mines, the coming of the railroad and the healthy aspects of Inyo's weather. The pamphlet stated, "We know of many cases of pulmonary, asthmatic and throat troubles that have been wonderfully benefitted, and in many cases absolutely cured." The same pamphlet also minimized the presence of alkali in the soil.

Figure 40-Water flowed in irrigation ditches throughout the Owens Valley before diversions began to take water to Los Angeles.

It's not clear just how much land was actually sold to "Friends" at the Quaker Colony, but according to a 1905 article in the *Inyo Register*, there were at least several dozen Quaker families who had chosen to come to Inyo to try their luck in what Mary Austin called the *Land of Little Rain*.

Most of those that came had been farmers in areas of the country that never needed to be irrigated. They worked hard but found the Owens Valley climate and soil not as favorable as had been promised in the promotional literature. Success and huge profits were not readily forthcoming.

In 1905, the city of Los Angeles began making offers to Owens Valley landowners to purchase their land and water rights. Though not clear about their intentions, the water was being obtained to send south in a new aqueduct the City was planning to build. Los Angeles was growing rapidly and believed it would need additional water if it were to continue to grow.

The City of Los Angeles quickly turned their attention to the land owned by the Quaker Colony and its farmers. The Colony's land and water rights holdings were huge. The "Friends" had grown tired of the challenges they faced, and very quickly became among the first to sell their land with its water rights to the thirsty southern California metropolis.

Despite the departure of the Quakers, the town of Owenyo continued as a railroad transfer point housing a number of railroad workers up through World War II. But the irrigation canals quickly dried up and the farms turned back into desert. The William Penn Colonial Association became another short-lived dream of fortune found…along El Camino Sierra.

CHAPTER FIFTEEN

WEDDING OF
THE WATERS

In 1937, there was not a more avid proponent of Eastern Sierra tourism than Catholic Priest Father John Crowley. Father Crowley had first come to the Owens Valley in 1919. His true-life story is told in detail in Chapter Two of *Tales Along El Camino Sierra*.

Crowley understood well the value of promotion. He knew the more attention one could obtain by getting his story told in the media, the more likely that story would become a success. One of his boldest publicity stunts was to climb Mt. Whitney in 1934, becoming the first and only priest known to have celebrated Mass at its summit.

The first road leading to Death Valley from the Lone Pine area was a toll road built by Stovepipe Wells founder Bob Eichbaum in 1926. The unpaved road was fairly primitive and was eventually taken over by the California Highway Department. The state rerouted, improved and paved the highway and Father Crowley quickly saw another opportunity to promote the region – not just in California, but throughout the nation.

Father Crowley said, "Many factors contributed to the possibility of a road dedication without precedent. For instance, not every road joins the top and bottom of a nation." The new link did just that, enabling motorists to drive in comfort and safety from Whitney Portal at the base of America's tallest peak, Mt. Whitney, to mysterious Death Valley and its below-sea-level reaches.

Father Crowley designed a three-day event he titled "The Wedding of the Waters." A gourd would be filled with water from Lake Tulainyo (one of the highest lakes in the contiguous United States at 12,820 feet) and would be transported by various means all the way to the opposite end of the new road, where the water would be poured into the Badwater Basin in Death Valley, the lowest spot in the U.S. at 282 feet below sea level.

Figure 41-The Badwater Basin in Death Valley, was the destination of the water that was brought from the lake near Mt. Whitney.

The event would be on a grand scale, involving not only the Governor of California but the President of the United States as well! Celebrities from Hollywood to the "real west" would partake in the pageant.

Jerry Emm, a Native American from Nevada was chosen to begin the saga. He was given the honor of dipping the gourd into the icy waters of Lake Tulainyo and running the first leg of the journey along the mountain trail descending to Whitney Portal, the terminus of the auto road.

At the Portal, Emm passed the gourd to local rancher Russell Spainhower, who dressed as a Pony Express rider, mounted his horse and galloped down the canyon. Five miles later, Spainhower handed the gourd to Ted Cook, another rider, who continued on horseback down the road. Seven miles further east, the gourd was given to Bert Johnson, the son of one of the men who first climbed Mt. Whitney. Astride his horse, Johnson carried the gourd through the streets of Lone Pine delivering it to actor William Boyd (known best as Hopalong Cassidy) who deposited the gourd in a vault at the bank for safekeeping until the next morning.

A fiesta was held that evening honoring Governor Frank Merriam and other state and national officials. A small amount of water from the gourd was prepared for the Governor to ceremoniously sip during the dinner.

Day two started early in the morning, with the governor standing on the steps of the bank and handing the water-filled gourd to Sam Ball, a long-time local prospector. Mr. Ball tied the gourd onto the back of his burro and walked south to the church where a covered wagon was waiting for the next leg of the journey. Aboard the wagon was Josephine Breen, a descendant of members of the ill-fated Donner Party. Pulled by two oxen, the wagon travelled two miles where it met up with a genuine Twenty-mule Team hitched to an original borax wagon. A mile later, the gourd was delivered to Ollie, the Mt. Whitney-Death Valley stagecoach driver who took it eight miles to where the new highway crossed the railroad tracks. Here train engineer Jim Henry placed the gourd in the cab of his locomotive and transported it to the railroad station in Keeler, where the gourd remained for the night.

Figure 42-The 20-Mule Team Wagon was brought out of retirement to carry the special gourd of water through the streets of Lone Pine.

On the final day, Father Crowley celebrated Mass on the church lawn in Lone Pine. When finished, he and others went to Keeler where the train was sitting at the station. The gourd was carried across the station platform and presented to Louie Meyer, a three-time winner of the Indianapolis 500 auto race. Meyer placed it in a brand new 1938 Lincoln Zephyr (a corporate sponsor) and sped away to the pass on the Argus Range, twenty-five miles away. At this spot waited Governor Merriam and a host of officials along with a temporary telegraph office set up by Western Union. Right on schedule, the wires clicked and with great celebration, the official signal was sent by President Franklin Roosevelt in Hyde Park, New York, commemorating the opening of the new highway. Governor Merriam fired a shotgun to announce the road was open.

Figure 43-Governor Frank Merriam fires a shotgun to signal the opening of the new road to Death Valley.

The Lincoln Zephyr, followed by a motorcade of hundreds of cars, wound down the steep road into Panamint Valley where an airplane waited to take the gourd on the final leg of its journey. Captain Carey, a veteran pilot from World War I took the water-filled gourd and flew off in his plane, flying over Telescope Peak and down into Death Valley, landing on an airfield at Furnace Creek. Carey then took off again, flew low over Badwater and emptied the gourd of water into the salty pool below.

As the droplets of mountain liquid rained down, a bonfire was lit and a pillar of flame shot up signaling to all those watching that the waters had "wedded" and the great Pageant had concluded. High above Badwater at Dantes View, a similar fire was lit which in turn was seen by the sentries across the valley on top of Telescope Peak. The Telescope Peak lookouts lit their bonfire, which was seen by those stationed on top of Cerro Gordo above Keeler, who signaled with their bonfire Norman Clyde, who was stationed atop Mt. Whitney. Norman lit the final fire as an indication to those gathered in Lone Pine, that the Pageant had ended. It was a grand heliograph of bon-fires signaling across the desert. As a final dramatic closing scene, Norman pushed the glowing embers off the face of Mt. Whitney in a symbolic recreation of the iconic Yosemite Fire Fall.

Figure 44-Indy 500 Winner Louie Meyer hands off the special gourd of water to World War I Flying Ace Captain Carey.

The crystal-clear water from one of America's highest lakes had been joined with the water of America's lowest lake. More importantly, Father Crowley's Wedding of the Waters was a gigantic marketing success. Hundreds of people took part celebrating this beautiful region and America's people from coast to coast had been exposed to the land of El Camino Sierra, an area that many knew nothing about prior to this historic and one of a kind event.

Did you know the
El Camino Sierra region is home to...?

- Mt. Whitney, the highest peak in the continental United States at 14,505 feet.
- The White Mountains, the highest desert mountain range in North America.
- Boundary Peak, the highest peak in the State of Nevada at 13,140 feet.
- The world's largest Jeffrey Pine Forest, located east of Mammoth Lakes and south of Mono Lake, directly along El Camino Sierra.
- The nation's first National Forest Scenic Area, the Mono Basin Scenic Area, designated in 1984.
- One of the oldest lakes in North America, Mono Lake, which has been determined to be at least 760,000 years.
- The world's oldest trees, the Bristlecone Pines of the Ancient Bristlecone Pine Forest located in the White Mountains. In 2012, a specimen was discovered to be over 5,000 years old.
- The nation's first designated Research Natural Area (RNA), the Harvey Monroe Hall RNA. Just east of Yosemite National Park and north of Tioga Pass, it was first established in 1933 to ensure the future of pristine ecosystems for scientific research.
- The Golden Trout, California's State Fish.
- The Mule Day's Parade, one of the largest non-motorized parades in the nation, held every Memorial Day weekend in Bishop.
- Inyo County, the second largest county in California and at 10,192 square miles, is larger than six states.
- More scenery that has appeared in Hollywood movies and television commercials than probably any other location in the United States, including urban cities.
- The Mono County Courthouse in Bridgeport, one of the oldest continually existing (and still used) courthouses in California.

CHAPTER SIXTEEN

DIRTY SOCK

No, the title of this chapter is not about finding someone's leftover laundry at the launderette, or wait…is it? Just off El Camino Sierra, about 5 miles northeast of the community of Olancha, is a little known location with this less-than-appealing name.

In 1917, the Santa Fe Pacific Railway (SFPR) (a subsidiary of the Atchison, Topeka and Santa Fe Railway) had plans to construct a soda plant on the southeast corner of shrinking Owens Lake. Owens Lake was disappearing due to diversions of the Owens River into an aqueduct completed by the City of Los Angeles in 1913.

The first step was for SFPR to drill a well to provide fresh water for the soda plant. At 600 feet, they struck a small amount of fresh water but would need more. They kept drilling and at 1,200 feet, hot water gushed forth from the well. Unfortunately, the water was highly mineralized and unsuitable as the freshwater source for the soda plant. SFPR abandoned its plans to construct the plant and despite its effort to plug the well, water has for the most part poured forth ever since.

Retired Darwin postmaster Oliver Thorsen eventually acquired the well and the property. In a 1964 letter to then Eastern California Museum Director Dorothy Cragen, Thorsen says he acquired the property from the SFPR in the 1940s.

Thorsen leased the property for a time to a developer that put in a huge 80-foot diameter concrete swimming pool and made other improvements purportedly costing $150,000. It was claimed, "Palm Springs would sit up and take notice" of the new resort the developer planned to build at Dirty Sock. These plans never moved much beyond constructing the large swimming pool at the well site.

There are a few different variations as to the source of the unflattering name. Some say it is because the aroma put off by the mineralized water smells like a dirty sock, or more correctly, many dirty socks. There is indeed quite a smell that has always come off the waters of Dirty Sock, but its source is actually the decomposition of the algae found here in the pool.

According to Thorsen, the origin of the name Dirty Sock is that once the well was abandoned, miners in the area would take their weekly (or monthly) bath at the well. At the conclusion of his bath, one miner noticed one of his socks had too many holes to put back on, so he left the "dirty sock" on a fence to help partly offset the odor from the rotting algae. Fellow miners seeing the hanging socked, dubbed the area "dirty sock."

Inyo County operated the springs as a County Park for a time in the 1960s, but the very unpleasant aroma kept (and still keeps) bathers away. The spring and pool are still there, but bathers are well served to consider enjoying one of the many other pleasant hot springs whose fragrance is more appealing and whose welcoming waters can be found…warming bathers along El Camino Sierra.

Figure 45-Dirty Sock Hot Springs was operated as an Inyo County Park for a time in the 1960s and '70s.

CHAPTER SEVENTEEN

LET'S HAVE A PICNIC

The Los Angeles Aqueduct was completed in 1913 and water from the Owens Valley began flowing south to slake the thirst of the growing metropolis. The Aqueduct was and still is a masterpiece of engineering, delivering water from the Owens River to Los Angeles, 233 miles away, entirely by gravity and siphon. No pumps are used to move the Aqueduct's water in its entire distance.

At first, Los Angeles acquired water rights primarily in the southern part of the Owens Valley. But as soon as Owens Valley water was delivered to the southland, the city's population exploded, creating a demand for yet more Owens Valley Water.

By 1920, Los Angeles began acquiring water rights in the Big Pine and Bishop areas. Some ranchers and farmers sold their land; others did not. Irrigation districts began to break apart over the sale of individual shares. The economy of the entire Owens Valley began to unravel under the strain of Los Angeles' unquenchable thirst.

Some angry citizens took to the extreme, dynamiting sections of the Aqueduct to at least temporarily stop the flow of water south. Los Angeles posted armed guards along the Aqueduct and instructed them to "shoot to kill" anyone who approached it.

On the evening of November 16, 1924, a leading Owens Valley banker led a group of approximately 70 Bishop and Big Pine men south down El Camino Sierra. They drove the highway with their headlights off to ensure they were not detected during their late-night foray.

Late in the evening, the group arrived at the Aqueduct's Alabama Gates, located just north of Lone Pine, and seized the diversion structure. The gates were opened and water flowed freely back into the Owens River, while the flow of water in the Aqueduct immediately dried up.

Los Angeles was outraged. After the City's attempts to get the local sheriff and judge to intervene on their behalf failed, Los Angeles pleaded unsuccessfully for assistance from neighboring county sheriffs. The City even asked the Governor of California to send in the National Guard to run off the occupiers.

The defiant group of Inyoites held on to the diversion gates for four days. Over 700 hundred Owens Valley residents joined the occupiers at the Gates. Women cooked meals and children played. The takeover was celebrated with a great community picnic. Western movie star Tom Mix, who was filming at the time in the nearby Alabama Hills, brought his film crew to the site to show solidarity with the protesters and also brought his band to keep the crowd entertained.

Figure 46-The LA Aqueduct ran dry when water bound for L.A. was diverted down the Alabama Gates back into the Owens River.

The occupiers eventually relinquished control of the Gates back to Los Angeles, but not before they had brought the attention of the world to the loss of their Valley's water and to the devestating effect it had on their socioeconomic well being.

The relationship between the City of Los Angeles and the Owens Valley remained strained for many years to come. The City continued to buy up Owens Valley land and water rights, and also implemented the pumping of valley groundwater from deep wells.

Figure 47-Water being released down the Alabama Gates back into the Owens River.

The citizens of the Owens Valley continued to express their outrage in a variety of ways, including persistent vandalizing of the Aqueduct. In one two-month stretch in 1927, at least seven instances of sabotage shook the Aqueduct. At one event, boxes of dynamite exploded inside the pressurized pipe of the No Name Canyon Siphon, causing it to burst. In another, saboteurs exploded a hillside bomb in an attempt to bury the aqueduct beneath a landslide.

As Los Angeles continued to grow, its unceasing demand for additional water continued. By 1941, the aqueduct system was extended all the way north to Mono Lake.

Los Angeles' diversion of four of the five creeks that feed Mono Lake caused it to shrink to half its size during the next few decades. Regulations and court orders have since been implemented attempting to keep Mono Lake at a level high enough to sustain a healthy ecosystem.

Figure 48-Damage to an LADWP siphon caused by saboteurs.

The City of Los Angeles now owns about 250,000 acres of land in Inyo County and another 60,000 acres in Mono County. It also controls nearly all of the water rights available in the Eastern Sierra south of Mono Lake.

The Los Angeles megalopolis versus two lightly populated counties several hundred miles away: an interesting, often difficult and sometimes confrontational relationship...found along El Camino Sierra.

CHAPTER EIGHTEEN

SEEMED LIKE A GOOD IDEA

Travelers motoring along El Camino Sierra, just a little south of Lone Pine can't help but notice the very pronounced scar of a road zigzagging its way up the eastern face of the Sierra Nevada. This is the Horseshoe Meadows Road, accessing some of the most sublime and lightly visited scenery in the Eastern Sierra.

This ominous looking roadway was blasted out of granite rock, giving it the very obvious "road-cut" look from afar. It's about 20 miles from the road's turnoff from the Whitney Portal Road, to road's end at beautiful Horseshoe Meadows. At 10,000 feet above sea level, this is the second highest paved road in California.

The first five miles of this road were built during the 1920s as a joint effort between Inyo County and the Los Angeles Department of Water & Power. The "City" was interested in the water and power potential of the Horseshoe Meadows area. The road-building technology at that time had not developed to the level needed for such serious mountain terrain and construction was soon halted.

The road remained only five miles in length until 1964, when work was resumed by Inyo County. The next 6.7-mile section took three summers and nearly $1.5 million of Federal Aid Secondary Highway money to complete. This new segment of road was still 1½ miles short of where the Horseshoe Meadows road ends today.

Horse packers have operated in the Horseshoe Meadows/Cottonwood Creek area since 1920. Golden Trout Camp, accessible only by trail, has hosted anglers, hunters and backcountry travelers in this area since that time as well.

The late 1960's was a time when government land managers were under direction to consider recreational opportunities wherever possible on their managed lands. Shortly after the Horseshoe Meadows Road was completed in 1967, the U.S. Forest Service issued a winter-sports development, special use permit to Southern Inyo Recreation Corporation. The company and the Forest Service planned to build a "moderate size" ski area at the west end of Horseshoe Meadows on Trail Peak.

Figure 49-The Horseshoe Meadows road climbs over 6,000' from the Owens Valley lowlands to some of the most sublime scenery in the Sierra.

In January 1972, it was announced Southern Inyo Recreation was having financial troubles and the proposed ski development was placed on hold. At the same time, the California Department of Fish and Wildlife, the Sierra Club and local citizens began to publicly express concerns about the scope of the proposed ski resort project. The Forest Service decided it prudent to re-evaluate its recreation plan for the Horseshoe Meadows area.

Through hearings, meetings and analytics, five separate alternatives were assembled for consideration. The least invasive of the alternatives was no development beyond what already existed in the Horseshoe Meadows area.

More hearings were conducted to gather additional public input. The alternatives were hotly debated with fully 55 percent of the comments favoring no additional development. A scaled down version was finally decided upon. The plan called for two walk in campgrounds, an equestrian campground, a pack station, hiker parking and access to numerous backcountry trails. No further development of the Horseshoe Meadows Road would take place.

Among the Forest Service's proposed alternatives for consideration during the hearing process was "Alternative V." According to the 1974 Forest Service *Horseshoe Meadows Land Use Plan* document, "this alternative resembles the original planned ski development previous to the decision to re-evaluate."

Among other things, this plan called for:
- A design that would accommodate 12,000 winter recreation visitors at one-time;
- Overnight accommodations for 2,600 visitors in winter and 3,800 in summer;
- Widening and improving the existing road;
- A large campground and interpretive facilities;
- Major gains in population and employment for Lone Pine and Olancha.

Figure 50-The wild landscapes of Horseshoe Meadows and Trail Peak were considered for a mega-ski resort in the 1960s.

Twelve thousand people a day, making their way up the steep and exposed Horseshoe Meadows Road in winter driving conditions seems like not just an absurdity but an impossibility. A well-spoken quote, "Sometimes the road less traveled is less traveled for a reason" may have been referring to the Horseshoe Meadows Road.

Today, the Horseshoe Meadows/Cottonwood Lakes area is one of the least visited areas in the southern Sierra Nevada Mountains. A weekday in the summer may see only a handful of people in the campgrounds and a few dozen cars at the trailhead. It is yet another of the many glistening jewels found in the Sierra Nevada.

We're all a product of our environment. What is an accepted practice in one decade may be the scourge of another. What appears to be sound thinking to one generation may reveal itself to be not so much so, a few years later. History teaches us it's not always prudent to rush to find fault with the ideas of others until we have "walked a mile in their shoes." Enjoy the Horseshoe Meadows/Cottonwood Lakes area of the Eastern Sierra, and appreciate the sublime and secluded treasure it still is…as it entices wilderness lovers of all ages as they travel…along El Camino Sierra.

CHAPTER NINETEEN

STEAMSHIPS OF SILVER

When driving El Camino Sierra along the edge of dry Owens Lake, it's difficult to envision that a great inland sea, 200 square miles in size, once lay here reflecting the magnificent Sierra Nevada in its beautiful deep blue waters. What is perhaps even more difficult to imagine is that large steamboats once plied its waters as well, transporting commerce across the lake to the various "ports" along its shore.

In 1872, the mining of silver at Cerro Gordo was going full steam. The mining camp was located high atop the Inyo Mountains southeast of Lone Pine and just northeast of Owens Lake.

Production of the precious ore became so great, it is said silver ingots were stacked up like cordwood to await shipment. James Brady, a superintendent of one of the Lake's silver smelting furnaces came up with the idea of bringing in a ship to help speed up the transport of ore across the Lake to waiting freight wagons. The steamship *Bessie Brady* arrived at Owens Lake in 1872 and immediately went to work.

Figure 51-Depiction of the *Bessie Brady* loading ore at Owens Lake.

The idea proved to be a good one. The *Bessie Brady* was able to make several trips a day, moving the silver ingots from the Lake's north shore to the Los Angeles bound freight wagons waiting on the south side near Cartago. A handful of other ships soon joined the effort to move the processed silver across Owens Lake.

The silver ore was refined and processed into bars or ingots at nearby smelters before being shipped south to Los Angeles. Shipping a purer product increased profits for investors. Kilns were constructed locally to produce the charcoal needed to operate the smelters.

Colonel Sherman Stevens began a wood and timber operation at Owens Lake west shore including a sawmill. Stevens provided needed timbers for the mines and cordwood for the charcoal kilns.

Seeing an opportunity, Stevens built his own steamship to haul lumber and charcoal across the lake to the mines and smelters. The Colonel christened his steamer the *Mollie Stevens* after his daughter. She made her maiden voyage across Owens Lake in June of 1877 and operated for the next few years.

The silver mines soon began to play out and the use of the steamship fleet began to wane. During a retrofit in 1882, the *Bessie Brady* caught fire and was consumed in flames. The short-lived use of steamships on Owens Lake came to an end almost as quickly as it had started.

Rumors (or legends) soon surfaced that when the *Bessie Brady* sank, she took with her to the bottom of the Lake $200,000 worth of bullion. Another incident was the alleged loss of a wagonload of bullion that was being carried on one of the steamers before its demise. The tale, originated by a man who said he heard it from the captain of the ship, contends the steamer was carrying two wagons loaded with bullion when one slipped off into the Lake. None of these lost riches have ever been found.

Back to Cottonwood Creek. This good size mountain stream originating in the alpine basin below 14,000 foot Mt. Langley, was used by Colonel Stevens as a mode of transportation to move logs 6,000 feet down the mountain from heavily forested Horseshoe Basin to his lumber mill below. Stevens constructed a log flume which proved a masterpiece of engineering, moving thousands of board feet of timber down an extremely steep slope, with virtually no major breakdowns. The milled lumber was mostly used for shoring up the Cerro Gordo mine tunnels as well as construction of its buildings.

Wood from Stevens's flume was also needed to make charcoal for the silver and lead smelters. Very hot fires were required to operate these smelters. Firewood would not burn hot enough, but charcoal would.

Two kilns made from mud were built by the west shore of Owens Lake and near the terminus of Stevens's log flume. These kilns provided the much-needed charcoal to process the valuable ore. The remains of these kilns can still be viewed today, accessed by a ½-mile dirt road off of Highway 395.

Figure 52-The log flume operated by Colonel Stevens was an efficient way to bring the lumber down from the High Sierra.

Though it's been over 140 years, evidence of Stevens's logging can still be seen today at Horseshoe Meadows. Numerous stumps are interlaced within the Meadow's beautiful Foxtail Pine forest.

Today of course, Owens Lake is not much more than a sand and dirt basin. Except for periods during extreme rainfall, the lake sits dry. But the story of stately steamships plying across a beautiful lake creates an enchanted image in one's mind...as they drive along this stretch of El Camino Sierra.

Figure 53-The Cottonwood Kilns produced charcoal for the Cerro Gordo smelters. Their remains can still be seen today, a half-mile off Highway 395.

Figure 54-Owens Lake full of water-photograph from approximately 1912.

CHAPTER TWENTY

NOT WHERE WE THOUGHT

The peaceful Bridgeport Valley is one of the most idyllic settings found along El Camino Sierra. With the jagged peaks of Yosemite's north country piercing the distant sky, and the verdant green meadows crisscrossed by a half dozen creeks, it's difficult to envision a more pastoral scene. But things have not always been so peaceful in this quaint and scenic mountain locale.

Figure 55-Sawtooth Ridge looms grandly over the Bridgeport Valley.

The mid 1800s were an exciting time throughout the western United States. With the discovery of gold in the foothills of the Sierra Nevada in 1848, tens of thousands of men and women left the East and Midwest to stake their claim to the easy riches they had read about in the newspapers, which were "supposedly" so easily attainable.

In 1859, the great Comstock Lode of Virginia City, Nevada was discovered and miners were quickly passing back across the Sierra Nevada. Not everyone "struck it rich." Most found nothing but the bottom of a worthless hole. Many of the discouraged prospectors headed over the next hill, hoping to find their long dreamed of bonanza.

In August of 1860, Joseph Wasson and others in his party were prospecting in the hills about 70 miles south of the Comstock. Silver was discovered and claims were quickly filed. Organizers were unsure if they were in California or Nevada Territory, but those on the scene declared it as California.

A town site was platted a month later named Aurora and by the spring of 1861 there were 2,000 inhabitants and an eight-stamp mill named the Pioneer, crushing ore.

Figure 56-Aurora grew almost overnight to upwards of 10,000 inhabitants.

When the State of California was first created, there were only 27 counties. As its population grew and demographics changed, new counties were created. Many of the "new" counties came about because of a discovery of precious metals far from established population centers. This area of Aurora was no exception.

In 1860, the western slope counties of Mariposa, Fresno and Calaveras stretched across the Sierra all the way to the Nevada border. With the

Aurora discovery of gold and silver, miners, prospectors and merchants wanted their own local government and petitioned the State to establish a new county called Mono, and of course, Aurora would be its county seat.

In April of 1861, Mono County was created and the mining camp of Aurora was indeed designated the seat of government. The town's good fortune seemed almost limitless as the population soon grew to nearly 10,000 residents and bragged of 16 mills processing ore.

Many Nevada Territory politicians weren't so sure that Aurora was actually in California and believed it may be on their side of the border. In fact, Nevada Territory soon claimed it as its own and Aurora became the county seat of Nevada's Esmeralda County. This made Aurora what is believed to be the only town to have been the county seat of two different counties, in two different states, at the same time. Its California assembly member was the speaker of the house while its Nevada legislative member was elected as president of the Nevada Territorial Legislature.

A survey team was jointly appointed by California Governor Leland Stanford and acting Nevada Territory Governor Orion Clemens, older brother of Samuel Clemens (Mark Twain), to establish the boundary once and for all. The town was so close to the oblique boundary line that its citizens didn't know for sure which side they were on. On Election Day 1863, just to be safe, they afforded themselves the privilege of voting as both Californians and Nevadans. If so inclined, a voter could cast a ballot for his favorite Californian at the police station, then walk down the street to the Armory Hall and do likewise as a citizen of Nevada Territory.

After the survey party passed through the area and performed their fiduciary duty, those favoring the Golden State, were disappointed. The survey had concluded Aurora lay three miles inside Nevada!

The Mono County politicians beat a hasty retreat west and quickly established Bridgeport as the new and legitimate county seat. The current courthouse was completed in 1881 and is one of the oldest continually occupied courthouses in California.

It has often been said, "Politics makes strange bedfellows." In the case of a disputed state boundary, politics can be very strange indeed, depending on where your bed was located. You'll find that can be especially so here…along El Camino Sierra.

Figure 57-The Mono County Courthouse in Bridgeport, since 1881.

"A mine is a hole in the ground, owned by a liar." Mark Twain.

CHAPTER TWENTY-ONE

ANCHORS AWEIGH...

In the 1950s, travelers heading to Tioga Pass, or Bodie, or any number of other Eastern Sierra locations, may have been surprised to see an enormous mushroom cloud of water shoot straight up out of Mono Lake, followed by a deafening boom.

At end of World War II, Americans were joyous with the expectation of finally having "peace at hand." However, no sooner were the peace treaties signed in Europe and Asia, the Cold War surfaced and became every bit as frightening and disconcerting as "real" war. Children practiced duck and cover drills in their classrooms, bomb shelters were constructed in back yards throughout the U.S. and Americans anxiously watched the latest world crisis on the new technology of television.

At the same time, GIs returning from Europe and Asia brought home a new level of sophistication with them and were ready to travel and "see America." Modern, affordable and comfortable cars were being produced by Detroit, and Americans were traveling in numbers never imagined.

The U.S. military was well intentioned in its mission to "protect" Americans from the looming menace of nuclear war. Scientists worked hand in hand with the military to develop the most advanced weapons and defense systems the world had ever seen.

In the 1950s, the U.S. military made their way to a number of remote locations, primarily in the western U.S., to conduct a wide variety of scientific experiments. The faraway reaches of Mono Lake made a perfect spot to conduct such tests.

The U.S. Navy detonated numerous huge explosions in the lake to determine the effect the blasts would have on generating large waves. Since Mono Lake had no fish, the military thought it would be a good spot to conduct such tests because the effects would be minimal. Due to public pressure, the Navy halted its testing in the early 1960s after several years of conducting "experiments" at Mono Lake.

Exactly what the U.S. Navy was trying to learn is still considered "Top Secret." A plaque noting this peculiar chapter of Mono Lake's history is located at the namesake of this experiment, Navy Beach. Today, this is one of the most popular destinations on Mono Lake, offering hiking, bird watching and canoeing. The Navy at Mono Lake? It did happen…and they traveled along El Camino Sierra to get there.

Figure 58-A plume of water rises from Mono Lake during a test conducted by the U.S. Navy in the 1950s.

CHAPTER TWENTY-TWO

THE PACK THAT WALKED LIKE A MAN

There are many legendary figures associated with the Sierra Nevada and Eastern California. John Muir traveled throughout its realm and was the first to refer to it as "the Range of Light." Ansel Adams called the Sierra Nevada home for several decades as he took some of his most iconic landscape photographs of its peaks, meadows and rivers.

But perhaps there is no one person that traveled so much of, and became so intimate with this extraordinary mountain range as a lightly known man of unsurpassed integrity and skill, Norman Clyde.

Clyde was born in Philadelphia, Pennsylvania in 1885. He spent a portion of his youth living in the wilds of Ontario, Canada where he successfully developed and fine-tuned his outdoor skills. Clyde obtained his college degree in the Classics before moving west, where he enrolled in the University of California Berkeley's graduate program. It was here Norman met the love of his life, Winifred Bolster.

After college, Clyde taught school in a number of locations while his wife worked as a nurse at a tuberculosis hospital. It was while there that Winnie contracted the awful disease herself, which led to her premature death in 1919 at the very young age of 28.

Winnie's death had a deep and profound effect on Clyde. He soon moved to the Eastern Sierra where he would spend much of the remainder of his life, alone in the mountains.

Clyde had already become an accomplished mountaineer before he met Winifred. He began climbing seriously shortly after he moved to California in 1910, spending months exploring and climbing in Yosemite and Sequoia. He wrote to his mother, "I have climbed the highest mountains in the region." In 1914, Norman joined the Sierra Club. In 1916, he ventured to the Mt. Shasta area, making the first of what would eventually be 12 ascents of this prolific peak. Clyde found himself at home in the mountains.

Figure 60-Norman Clyde spent every moment he could in the mountains he loved.
Shortly after his wife's death, Clyde accepted a job as the teaching/principal of the school in Independence. The position was perfect for Clyde. He could spend every weekend and all summer in the Sierra Nevada exploring and climbing. He would often lead Sierra Club trips during the summer months.

Clyde quickly honed his mountaineering and climbing skills to a level unknown and unrivaled among climbers of his time. He began to look for new routes to the summit of peaks (called first ascents). He returned to Mt. Shasta in 1923 where he set a speed record by ascending over 6,100 feet to its summit in just over three-hours. That same summer he climbed 36 peaks in 36 days in Glacier National Park, Montana, eleven of them first ascents.

In 1925, Clyde made 53 ascents in the Sierra Nevada and told fellow climber Francis Farquhar that, "I sometimes think I climbed enough peaks this summer to render me a candidate for a padded cell—at least some people look at the matter in that way. However, I get a lot of enjoyment from this rather strenuous form of diversion."

Figure 61-Norman Clyde became legendary for his climbing skills.

In 1928, Clyde was a leader of a Sierra Club trip to the Canadian Rockies. The Mazamas from Oregon and the Mountaineers from Washington, two highly respected outdoor clubs joined them. It was during that trip that Clyde came to the realization that making a living by being in the mountains was what he really wanted to do with his life. He traversed the entire San Gabriel Mountain Range of southern California. He later made a headline-grabbing trip from the summit of Mt. Whitney to the Badwater Basin in Death Valley, all from sunrise to sunset on a single day.

Clyde soon got his wish to have more time in the mountains. One day during the 1929 school year, Clyde heard vandals were going to do bad deeds upon the school in Independence. Clyde hid in the evening darkness waiting for the wayward students to appear. Exactly what happened next is not completely clear. What is known is that the students showed up and, before the incident was over, fresh bullet holes appeared in the fender of their car. The parents of the students asked Norman to resign his position the next day.

Over the next four decades, Clyde climbed thousands of peaks and led an even greater number of trekkers and outdoor lovers on hundreds of hiking, climbing and mountaineering trips. Clyde also became a prolific writer, publishing articles in numerous magazines and periodicals. Several of his articles were later combined and made into a book titled *Close Up of the High Sierra.*

Clyde became friends and climbing partners with some of the best mountaineers of the day including Peter Starr, Francis Farquhar, Jules Eichorn, Lewis Clark, Bestor Robinson and Glen Dawson. Over his lifetime, Clyde is credited with having made at least 130 first ascents on various peaks; mostly in the mountains he loved so much, the Sierra Nevada. His many climbing achievements are still unrivaled and unchallenged to this day.

Clyde's climbing skills and in-depth knowledge of the mountains led to him being called upon numerous times to assist with mountain rescues. Clyde was a humble man and would have never dreamed of keeping track of the number of times he led a search and rescue/recovery, or the number of people whose lives he saved. Those that knew him estimated it numbered in the hundreds.

Clyde was never one to leave anything behind when he ventured into the mountain backcountry. Among the contents of his enormous backpack would be a selection of hardbound books (the *Classics* of course), as many as five different cameras, and a hammer and cobbler's anvil in order to make repairs to his and others' hiking boots while in the backcountry. He became known by all as "the pack that walked like a man."

Figure 62-Norman Clyde became known as the "Pack that walked like a man" because of the huge loads he would carry.

As the years passed and Clyde began to slow down, he became the caretaker at historic Glacier Lodge, located at the end of the Big Pine Canyon Road. He made his final trip into the mountains at age 85, over the Sierra crest to Fourth Recess on Mono Creek.

Truly, no one person has cared so much for, spent so much time in, and helped to expose so many people to, the Sierra Nevada than Norman Clyde. Rarely has so little been written about someone of Clyde's gargantuan stature. But then again, that would be just the way humble Clyde would want it, here where he was always at home…along El Camino Sierra.

Figure 63-Legendary Sierra Mountaineer Norman Clyde.

CHAPTER TWENTY-THREE

YELLOWSTONE IN THE SIERRA

The Eastern Sierra has some of the most diverse geology to be found anywhere. Faulting, uplifting, glaciations and volcanism are just a few of the geologic processes readily apparent as one motors along El Camino Sierra.

The Sierra Nevada is home to the most southerly glacier, the tallest mountain peak and the deepest valley in the U.S. The area along its eastern slope is also home to several active geothermal areas. From the volcanic fields at Little Lake and Red Hill to the Craters at Mono Lake, it's obvious that there's been a few "hot spots" underground here in the Eastern Sierra.

Hot springs have long been a popular destination for visitors to the area and still are today. Evidence shows that Native Americans have been using these natural hot and warm waters for thousands of years and still consider the sites sacred.

Hot springs resorts along El Camino Sierra have been in operation almost since the first tourists arrived. Their first use was thought to have been for medicinal and healing purposes, but it's doubtful anyone has ever refuted that they also just "felt good" to sit in and relax.

These geothermal areas can have many other benefits as well. Often, when there are hot springs there are also areas of steam. If there is enough of it, steam can be used to generate electricity. Two of the largest geothermal generating plants in California are found in Inyo and Mono Counties.

Just north of Little Lake in southern Inyo County, is the turnoff for the Coso Geothermal area. Partially on land now owned by the U.S. Navy, these hot springs have been used as a sacred ceremonial site by Native Americans for centuries. The first written accounts of the area talked about "thousands of hot mud springs of all consistencies and colors" and referred to the area as Hot Sulphur Springs.

In 1895, William Grant took deed to the land and opened a health resort a few years later. Claims were made that the waters and mud could cure everything from venereal disease to constipation. The water and mud were sold at high prices while touting to provide "Volcanic Health and Beauty from Nature's Great Laboratory." At first, Coso Hot Springs Resort only drew local residents, but as traffic along El Camino Sierra increased and the highway improved, tourists from southern California and the San Francisco Bay area came to Coso to be cured. In 1943, the U.S. Navy took over the resort and most of the geothermal area as it expanded its China Lake Naval Ordnance Test Station and closed the area to the public.

Figure 64-Coso Hot Springs was a popular health resort from 1909 until 1943.

In cooperation with the Navy, the Coso geothermal area has been producing electricity from steam since the mid-1980s. Today, the facilities produce enough electricity to power 145,000 homes in California on an average day. Tours of the area are occasionally available through the Maturango Museum in Ridgecrest, California.

Traveling further north on El Camino Sierra, travelers encounter numerous ancient volcanic flows, especially in the area between Independence and Big Pine. Black jagged lava fields can be seen spreading out from both the Inyo and Sierra Nevada sides of the Owens Valley. Crater Mountain is one of the larger old volcanoes found in the area.

Further north, near the intersection of El Camino Sierra and Hwy 203 leading into the town of Mammoth Lakes, is the Casa Diablo Hot Springs. Native Americans also used these hot springs for hundreds of years, building shelters over the springs to take their soakings. Later, small cabins were erected providing baths for prospectors and travelers. The spot also served as a stage stop and supply point for commerce headed to the mines near Mammoth. They named the area Casa Diablo or "House of the Devil" for the many boiling hot springs.

In the early 1900s, Charlie Summers purchased the hot springs and 40 acres of adjacent land. Sometime around 1920, the family constructed a small resort at the spot, which included a fuel station, dining room, bar and even a dance hall. The friendly resort was another one of many welcomed sites for travelers along El Camino Sierra.

Figure 65-Casa Diablo Resort was located near the turnoff for Mammoth Lakes.

Casa Diablo is unique among Eastern Sierra geothermal areas in that it was once home to an erupting geyser. The Casa Diablo Geyser would have held its own against the famous Yellowstone thermal gushers. However, the geyser apparently did not erupt with any real regularity. It would lie dormant for long periods and then burst forth with a rousing eruption. During the 1930s, the geyser would shoot as high as 70 to 80 feet.

Today, Casa Diablo is home to a geothermal plant that provides enough electricity for over 30,000 homes. The geyser is gone but the special memories of a boiling fountain erupting along the base of the Sierra Nevada, still remains in the pictures and scrapbooks of travelers from long ago as the relive their "warm" memories...from along El Camino Sierra.

Figure 66-The now dormant Casa Diablo Geyser would erupt with a fountain of hot water 70' to 80' high.

CHAPTER TWENTY-FOUR

BIG TREE OF BIG PINE

Travelers passing through Big Pine on El Camino Sierra can't help but notice the magnificent conifer tree at the intersection of Highways 395 and 168. Because of the tree's prominence in the town, it is often thought that it must be the eponym of Big Pine, but not so. The tree is not a pine at all, but a Giant Sequoia.

When European settlers first arrived, the creek flowing from the mountains through their farms had several Jeffrey Pines lining its banks. The story told is that one by one the trees were cut down until only one remained. The town of Big Pine was named after this last remaining tree though it too was later cut down, to make room for a service station.

Today the Giant Sequoia sits like a lonely sentinel on the town's northeast side. The enormous tree looms above all others and can be easily seen as one motors into Big Pine. The tree is known as the Roosevelt Tree.

It is reported that the Roosevelt Tree was planted in July of 1913, to commemorate the opening of Westgard Pass (Hwy 168) to automobile traffic. Though no longer in office at the time of the planting, the tree was named in honor of President Theodore "Teddy" Roosevelt.

The Giant Redwood, or Sequoiadendron giganteum as it is called in the scientific world, is not native to the Eastern Sierra. This most magnificent of all conifers inhabits the western slope of the Sierra Nevada from east of Sacramento to south of Sequoia National Park, at elevations ranging from 5,000 to 8,000 feet.

Several specimens of this monarch exist along El Camino Sierra outside of Big Pine. Mature Giant Sequoias inhabit the towns of Lone Pine, Independence and Bishop. The two tallest trees in Independence (at the County Courthouse and at the former Los Angeles Department of Water & Power's headquarters) are both of this noble species.

The Roosevelt Tree in Big Pine is only slightly over 100 years old, yet looms well over 100 feet in height. It appears that even though these monoliths are not native, they find life quite to their liking …growing stately along El Camino Sierra.

Figure 67-The Roosevelt Tree in Big Pine shortly after being planted in 1913.

CHAPTER TWENTY-FIVE

OWENS VALLEY IRON HORSE

Today, commerce moves along El Camino Sierra to destinations throughout the northern and western parts of the United States. Large semi-trucks are a fairly common sight along this most scenic ribbon of blacktop.

Many years ago, dirt roads, remoteness and lack of services made moving goods and supplies by truck and auto, a difficult task. But a fairly efficient transportation system arrived in Eastern California towards the end of the 19th century, and the movement of products and people became much easier.

The silver boom was well under way on the Comstock of Northern Nevada in the 1870s. The Virginia and Truckee (V&T) Railroad serviced Virginia City, Gold Hill, Carson City and eventually Reno during this time. At the peak of the great silver boom, the V&T operated 30 to 45 trains a day between Carson City and Virginia City. The railroad boasted of 22 locomotives and 361 freight cars, and was turning a profit of over $100,000 a month in 1870s dollars.

Spurred by the profits being made from its involvement in mining towns, the V&T executives made a decision in 1880 to build a new railroad, south past Hawthorne, Nevada, into California over Montgomery Pass and down through the Owens Valley. To save expense, it would be a "narrow gauge" railroad, with tracks only thirty-six inches apart compared to a standard gauge's fifty-six inch width. The new line was built to take advantage of the mining boom happening at the time in Bodie as well as smaller strikes at Candelaria, Nevada and Bend City and San Carlos in the Owens Valley.

The new line was named the Carson & Colorado Railroad (CCRR) though it was never the intention to run the railroad as far as the state of Colorado. Rather, it was planned to someday run to the mines near the Colorado River in Nevada and Arizona.

The line extended as far as Candelaria by 1882, and all the way to Keeler (300 miles) on the shores of Owens Lake by July of 1883. The "Slim Princess" as it was called, brought supplies into Eastern California and hauled goods, people and ore out.

The narrow-gauge railroad didn't turn the profits its investors had hoped for. The mining activity in the area fluctuated wildly and though people did use the rail line for travel to and from the Owens Valley, it was not easy to do so. The tracks for the Carson & Colorado ran along the east side of the Owens Valley, while the major towns were all on the west.

As the fortunes of the V&T waned, it sold its CCRR line to the Southern Pacific Railroad (SP). Good fortune fell right in the SP's lap when in the very early 1900s, gold and silver were discovered in Goldfield and Tonopah, Nevada. The strikes were promising and the SP elected to replace the narrow gauge with a standard gauge from Carson City to Mina, Nevada, where it connected to the new Tonopah Railroad. The existing line into the Owens Valley was left a narrow gauge.

Figure 68-Engine 18 was one of the narrow-gauge locomotives that operated in the Owens Valley. It is now on display in Independence.

In 1910, the Southern Pacific built a standard gauge line into the Owens Valley from southern California, primarily to support the construction of the Los Angeles Aqueduct. The new standard gauge met the narrow gauge at Owenyo (the former Quaker Colony town).

Over the next five decades, the use of the Carson & Colorado continued to decline. In the 1940s, the line from Laws (near Bishop) north was torn out. The narrow gauge was left operating only between Laws and Owenyo, and not very often.

In late spring of 1954, MGM Studios announced they would be filming a new movie on location in the Lone Pine area. The movie was titled *Bad Day at Bad Rock* and starred Spencer Tracy, Anne Francis, Robert Wagner, Lee Marvin and Walter Brennan. MGM would build a faux town near the old Lone Pine railroad depot for the movie. The studio also worked out a deal with the Southern Pacific Railroad to bring one of its super modern Streamliner passenger trains up from L.A. to be used in the movie.

MGM wanted two diesel locomotives and five modern passenger cars for the scene and it was reported SP charged MGM $5,500 and the cost of 265 round-trip passenger tickets for use of the trains.

Due to the weight of the train and the fact that the tracks in the Lone Pine area were constructed for smaller and lighter freight trains, there was a fair amount of concern whether the train could make it up to Lone Pine safely. Bridges were approached with the lighter passenger cars first and the heavier engines trailing, in case a bridge collapsed. The 200-mile trip from southern California to Lone Pine took twelve hours as the train never traveled faster than 25 miles an hour.

Figure 69-Southern Pacific passenger train in movie Bad Day at Black Rock.

The last train operated in the Owens Valley in 1960. Local school children and residents were invited to ride the last trip of this vestige of Eastern California history. But residents weren't about to let this piece of their heritage just fade away. Community members in Independence obtained one of the old CCRR steam locomotives for display at the County park and folks in Bishop obtained another of the historic iron horses for display and public enjoyment at Laws Railroad Museum.

Independence's Engine #18 has recently been restored to working condition by a dedicated group of volunteers. As of early 2017, this treasured piece of Eastern California history is being moved to a new location at the Eastern California Museum for display, and for the enjoyment for all those traveling and dreaming of days of yesteryear that have taken place...along El Camino Sierra.

Figure 70-Engine 18 is set be placed on display at the Eastern California Museum in Independence by the Spring of 2017.

CHAPTER TWENTY-SIX

KEOUGH HOT SPRINGS

For over a century, Keough Hot Springs has been another one of those "institutions" found along El Camino Sierra. Prior to the arrival of white settlers, the hot springs had been an important piece of Native American culture for hundreds of years.

The hot springs were part of two different ranching operations: the Longyear family and the 4-C Ranch. Early Owens Valley settlers, including both pioneer families, found the hot waters relaxing and rejuvenating, much the same as visitors to Keough do today.

In 1919, Bishop businessman and community leader Phillip Keough purchased the property. He had a vision to turn the hot springs into a world-class health resort.

Figure 71-Keough's warm waters have been soothing bathers for centuries.

Keough put in a swimming pool, soaking tubs, a dining room, dance hall and cabins. During the 1920s and '30s, it was "the" place to be, for locals and tourists alike. It was not just the hot springs that drew people; it became a social gathering spot and an entertainment destination as well.

Holidays were celebrated at Keough's with great fanfare. Barbecues, dancing and fireworks marked 4th of July celebrations. A huge Easter egg hunt on the Keough Resort grounds attracted hundreds of children from throughout the Valley.

The young men from the Civilian Conservation Corp camp near Lone Pine would come to Keough for dances and sometimes a ballgame. Schools in Bishop and Big Pine held end of school year parties, where many a young Inyoite learned to swim in the Resort's heated pool. Boxing matches were sometimes staged at Keough's and even Hollywood movie stars would visit for vacation getaways.

The City of Los Angeles eventually purchased the property as part of its land grab in the 1930s. Los Angeles leased the resort to private operators, but with only short-term leases being offered, Keough's went into a period of closures and reduced operations.

In 1955, renovations took place restoring some of Keough's former glory. In 1998, long time Bishop family, the Browns, purchased Keough's and have conducted major remodeling and improvements. Today Keough's still features its famous pool as well as a snack bar, picnic area and massage therapy. Visitors and locals alike are still enjoying a relaxing time in these rejuvenating waters flowing warming…along El Camino Sierra.

Figure 72-Swimmers enjoy a dip in Keough's large swimming pool.

CHAPTER TWENTY-SEVEN

SHERWOOD FOREST

Figure 73-A brochure from the 1960s.

Travelers along El Camino Sierra whose memories include bell-bottoms and Watergate, just might remember this little known 1960s-70s gem of a tale as well.

Sherwood Forest was located on the eastside of Hwy 395 at the Fort Independence Reservation. Sherwood Forest was actually a petting zoo that harbored a number of animals for kids and their parents to come see and feed. It didn't seem to make any difference to the visitors that none of the animals were native to the Eastern Sierra.

Squirrel monkeys, Corsica Mountain Sheep, llamas and Wallaroos all found themselves a comfortable home at the Forest. Even the deer were brought all the way from Europe.

Russ Hamilton built Sherwood Forest in the late 1950s. He had operated another successful "Forest" in Cave Rock, Oregon before he made his way south to

Eastern California. Hamilton sold the operation about 1969 to a local family that kept it running up until the late 1970s. The Hamiltons opened another Deer Park near Williams, Arizona that is still open today.

Oak Creek dropped over a small waterfall as it wound its way through the property, while the likeness of Jack and Jill, the Three Little Pigs and Little Boy Blue bid welcome to the guests. Food was available for the tourists to feed to the animals.

Popular with travelers as well as locals, the Forest was a fairly low key operation, usually employing just family members. A 1960s-era brochure states the price was .75 cents for adults and .25 cents for children. The brochure also boasts of a "Modern Souvenir Shop which contains one of the finest selections in the Eastern High Sierra."

One of the great things people enjoy while traveling on the magic ribbon of blacktop known as Highway 395 are the many fond memories they take home with them. The Sherwood Forest: another little-known tale and producer of lifelong memories, gone, but not to be forgotten...along El Camino Sierra.

Fig 74-Visitors to Sherwood Forest feed the many animals circa 1960.

CHAPTER TWENTY-EIGHT

FISH ON!

Arguably, even before the first automobile motored down El Camino Sierra, fishing has been the mainstay of Eastern California tourism. People today may come to hike, ski, sightsee and take photographs…but angling for that "big one" in the clear waters of the Sierra Nevada still attracts hundreds of thousands of people every year.

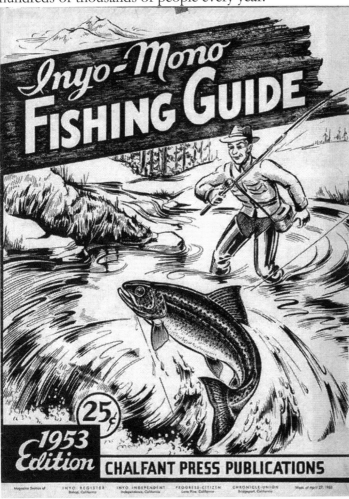

Figure 75- Fishing has played a large role in the Eastern Sierra's economy since the first tourist motored up El Camino Sierra.

However, if it weren't for the hard work and commitment of a select handful of foresighted people, sport fishing may never have even got off the ground in the Counties of Inyo and Mono.

Trout are not native to the Eastern Sierra. In 1872, J.W. McMurry from Big Pine brought two dozen rainbow trout from the Kings River on the Sierra Nevada Western slope, and planted them in a reservoir on his property near Fish Springs in the Owens Valley. Additionally, Inyo County pioneer A.A. Brierly told of one A.W. Robinson who arrived in Independence in 1872 and was disappointed to find only suckers and chubs in the local waters. Brierly stated that Robinson made the trip over Kearsarge Pass to Bubbs Creek, also on the west slope of the Sierra Nevada. It was here Robinson caught an unknown number of trout and brought them back and planted them in Independence Creek.

The excitement of the possibility of establishing a trout fishery in the Owens Valley led to the announcement in the *Inyo Independent* newspaper, July 26, 1873 that, "It is hoped that for the next two years any individual disturbing them (the trout) will be immediately reduced to bait for the benefit of the fish remaining."

Over the next few decades, dozens of fish entrepreneurs brought fish (primarily trout) from a variety of areas back to Inyo and Mono waters to help establish what would one day become a flourishing fishery. Catfish were brought from Reno and planted in the Owens River. Perch were also introduced to local waters.

The establishment of a sport fishery in the Eastern Sierra wasn't without its challenges. In 1884, after years of growth, the fish population in a number of local creeks began to decline. For reasons not clear, the Nevada Fish and Game Commission crossed state lines and planted 6,000 brook and rainbow trout in the waters near Bishop. The Nevada folks returned in 1888 to plant an additional 7,000 trout in Big Pine Creek.

Gradually the fishery began to take hold in the area's creeks, rivers and lakes. Newspaperman Willie Chalfant observed in an editorial, "Fish are said to afford the greatest amount of brain nutrients, therefore there will be no risk of an undue percentage of idiots among the rising and future generations of Owens Valley people."

Figure 76-Fishing the area lakes and creeks have drawn millions of visitors over the years to the Eastern Sierra Nevada.

Local clubs sprang up whose purpose was to promote fishing in their respective areas. The Golden Trout Club from Lone Pine worked to make sure not only Golden trout but also Rainbow trout were kept well populated in creeks from Olancha to Big Pine. The Rainbow Club from Bishop worked tirelessly for decades, promoting sport fishing to anglers far and wide.

An April 13, 1922 edition of the *Inyo Register* ran an article with headlines "RAINBOW DAY TO BE DULY OBSERVED BY OUR SPORTSMEN." The article states there is no more enthusiastic of an organization than the Rainbow Club. It boasts of the Club managing local campgrounds and conducting fishing tournaments.

Noted Sierra Nevada mountaineer and outdoorsman Norman Clyde is quoted in 1929 as saying, "One can stand on any peak along the crest of the Sierra in Inyo and Mono counties and close his eyes, turn around three times and in that direction will be found lakes and streams well stocked with trout—gold, rainbow, eastern brook and Loch Leven varieties."

Figure 77-The Rainbow Fishing Club was instrumental in promoting trout fishing in the Eastern Sierra.

"Eastside" folks seemed to have a special knack for promotion. From W. Gillette Scott to Father John Crowley…they made sure people knew just how great visiting (and fishing) the Eastern Sierra could be.

A November 1919 article in the *Owens Valley Herald* reports on the Fish and Game Commission's "fishing exhibit" at the recent California State Fair and how it was, "The biggest attraction at the fair." The article describes a cyclorama of the Sierra Nevada with a miniature Mt. Whitney looming in the south, and an equal pint sized version of the Mt. Whitney Fish Hatchery a bit to its north. A portion of the exhibit also contained, "A large aquaria filled with the famous Golden trout of the Mt. Whitney region."

It's likely sport fishing along El Camino Sierra may have never attained the level of popularity it has without the support and hard work of these fishing clubs. Starting in 1921, the Rainbow Fishing Club would erect a "fish display" every Rainbow/Fishing Opening Day. Anglers could "show off" their prized catches for public viewing at these displays that would often feature hundreds of fish.

Beginning shortly after the Mt. Whitney Fish Hatchery was opened in 1918; the Rainbow Club members were responsible for planting over 5 million fish, mostly on foot, in 55 lakes and 25 streams in Inyo and Mono Counties. All this in just the first eight years of the hatcheries existence! Their boast to prospective members was that they would plant 1,000 fish for every $1 Rainbow Club membership fee paid.

By the early 1940s, Black Rock and Fish Springs hatcheries were built in the Owens Valley. After World War II, the demand for sport fishing exploded. With many skilled pilots returning from the War and an available surplus of airplanes, the Fish and Game Commission turned to planting fish in the Sierra backcountry from the air.

Figure 78-Planting fish by hand was extremely labor intensive. After WW II, the Department of Fish & Game turned to airplanes to bring fish to the High Sierra lakes.

The Blake Jones Fishing Derby is one of the highlights of the fishing season in the Eastern Sierra. Held in mid-March every year since 1968, the Derby is a blind bogey event with a multitude of ways to win. In 2016, over $10,000 in prizes were awarded.

The Derby is named in honor of a man who helped put Bishop on the fishing map and who also invented the modern-day cheese bait. Blake Jones and his wife Peggy were both legendary anglers of the Sierra Nevada waters. Fact of the matter is Peggy would often out-fish Jones.

Jones and Peggy were equally well known for their hospitality, and willingness to help fellow anglers. They were the type of people that would never hesitate to stop along the road and help someone fish. Maybe give them some of their special bait or suggest a better location.

One of Jones lasting legacies is his creation of bottled cheese bait that would actually stay on the hook. He came up with the concept and sold his product throughout the Sierra. It was his idea that is credited with the later creation of Berkley Power Bait style of flavored baits.

Jones and Peggy became the Eastern Sierra's biggest promoters of sport fishing. He would attend tradeshows throughout California and then work

with local packers to ensure anglers would have the best time possible once they arrived. He would guide for sport and travel writers and worked with several fishing programs. Blake Jones passed away in 1987. His legacy continues along El Camino Sierra, in the Fishing Derby that bears his name…and with the Sierra fish that still fear him.

Figure 79-Legendary Bishop fisherman Blake Jones.

CHAPTER TWENTY-NINE

MIDLAND TRAIL

By 1910, the entire nation had worked itself up into a fervor regarding the building and development of roads throughout the country. It wasn't just El Camino Sierra that was garnering the attention of W. Gillette Scott and the Inyo Good Roads Club. Scott had his sights on other proposed Inyo County routes as well.

Highways that would link the east and west coasts of the U.S. held just as much interest as local roads. In 1911, Charles Davis from Kentucky formed the National Highways Association (NHA). Their slogan was "Good Roads Everywhere" but their primary interest was creating national roadways.

Federal Highway Administration Director Logan Page appointed NHA Vice-president Anton Westgard to research possible routes across the United States to build a transcontinental highway. Several routes were to be considered. Westgard and his group headed west in 1913 to begin their work.

Towns clamored for Westgard and his group's attention as they conducted their research. A transcontinental highway running through a community could make the difference between prosperity and poverty. In an effort to lure interest away from the preferred Salt Lake City to Reno route, Goldfield, Nevada and Big Pine invited Westgard and the research party to festivities held in their towns to promote their respective communities.

Supporters of El Camino Sierra knew an opportunity when they saw one. In order to curry the Association's favor, W. Gillette Scott and the Inyo Good Roads Club named the route across the gap between the Inyo and White Mountains, Westgard Pass in honor of their "distinguished guest."

The official transcontinental highway, which was to become known as the Lincoln Highway, ended up following the Salt Lake to Reno route. But all was not lost. The Midland Trail, as the Westgard Pass route was called, would run from Washington D.C. to Big Pine, with variations to the north and south. For a time, the Midland Trail actually became the more traveled route, since the Lincoln Highway over Donner Summit was closed for several months each winter due to snow, while Westgard Pass remained mostly snow free. Westgard himself described this route as an "impressive gateway into California."

Though the official Midland Trail in California is now long gone, State Highway 168 winds its way over scenic Westgard Pass to many beautiful sights, and scenes of history. This historic trail boasts not only of the many tales from the past...but of the many tales from the present...and they all start and end...along El Camino Sierra.

Figure 80-The original Midland Trail ran from Washington D.C. to Big Pine. The Auto Club of southern California placed thousands of highway signs throughout the west during the nation's early years of road building.

CHAPTER THIRTY

POWER TO BODIE

Bodie is one of the most historic areas to be found along El Camino Sierra. There are many stories (and a few myths) that are tied to this old mining town (now a California State Park). A common told tale about Bodie concerns it being the first location that electricity traveled a significant distance over power lines. Though the tale is not quite accurate, it is still an interesting one.

In 1876, the Standard Mining Company discovered a rich lode of gold at Bodie, California and another mining rush was underway. Prospectors and miners made their way to the lofty 8,400-foot isolated town by the thousands. Unlike many boomtowns, Bodie's ore veins ran fairly deep and the town prospered for well over a decade.

Many new lodes were discovered, but the Standard Company's mines remained the largest. The superintendent of the Standard Company was Thomas Leggett. By the early 1890s, ore deposits were starting to dwindle and though the Standard was still making money, operational costs were huge and Leggett sought to improve the company's bottom line by reducing milling expenses. Cordwood was the fuel used to power the steam engines that ran the stamp mill and it was costing the Standard over $22,000 a year (that's almost $500,000 in today's dollars.) for fuel. Leggett was desperate to reduce his power costs.

The use of electricity for commercial purposes had rapidly developed in the 1880s. George Westinghouse and Nikola Tesla had discovered that alternating current (AC) could be economically transmitted over long distances with the use of transformers. The Standard's Leggett took notice and decided to build a powerhouse on Green Creek about 12.5 miles from his mill. Legend is that Leggett was concerned the electricity would fly off any bends in the lines. The transmission lines were erected in a fairly straight line from the dynamo to the mill with just a few minor jogs on the way. However, in a profile view the lines definitely were not straight.

There were many dips and peaks as the lines crossed gullies and hills on its route to Bodie. The electric power current arrived "safely" in Bodie.

By the time Leggett's power plant began to operate, electricity had already been transmitted over lines as much as 29-miles in length, at various locations in the U.S. and Europe. There was great excitement and relief when the transmission at Green Creek was successful, but it is doubtful the engineers were ever really worried it wouldn't work.

Figure 81-(above) The Green Creek Power Plant 1893.
Figure 82-(below) The intake pond for Green Creek Power Plant.

CHAPTER THIRTY-ONE

MONO LAKE MEMORIES

Mono Lake is one of those magical places that lives on in people's memories long after their visit has ended. Not only is it one of the most scenic spots on the entire El Camino Sierra, its human history contains some of the most interesting tales to be found.

Parts of Mono Lake's human history are well known. The true story of the city of Los Angeles diverting four of the five streams that fed the Lake and its subsequent dropping of 40 vertical feet in just 54 years, set in motion a great awareness of water usage and conservation throughout the world.

Other parts of Mono's human history, though deep and rich, are not as well known. The Kutzadika'a People are the predecessors of the current day Mono Lake Paiute. Native Americans have been living an abundant life along the shores of one of North America's oldest lake for hundreds of years.

As with all lands throughout the American West, things began to change once the white settlers arrived in the mid-1800s. In 1857, gold was discovered a few miles north of Mono Lake at Dogtown; at nearby Monoville in 1859 and Aurora, Nevada in 1860. In just a matter of a few years over 10,000 people lived at or near Mono Lake. The Native American way of life was forever changed.

Wallis D. McPherson moved to the Mono Basin with his wife Venita in 1909. They were innovative, industrious and hardworking folks, who became involved in several different business ventures over the next 20 years in the Mono Basin.

McPherson worked for the local irrigation ditch company and spent his off time exploring the Mono Basin and its secrets. He had particular interest in Pahoa, the large white island of Mono Lake. The island had hot springs and a fair amount of developable land. Wallis thought it had the potential to become a first-class health resort.

McPherson acquired over 360 acres on Pahoa where he soon built a home and raised corn, goats, and their son Wallis R (Wally) McPherson. Wallis senior partnered with a southern California investor and together they acquired an additional 135 acres on the "mainland" along the west shore of Mono Lake.

Figure 83-The McPherson's homestead on Pahoa Island.

McPherson and his partner planned to not only build the health resort on Pahoa Island, they also intended to construct a 100-room hotel on their mainland property for their guests to stay at while visiting the health spa.

McPherson bought an excursion boat to take the visitors and spa guests out to Pahoa Island. The boat, aptly named the *Pahoa,* was built in San Pedro and shipped via rail to the Mono Basin via the Carson & Colorado Railway (see Chapter 25).

Once Wally became of school age, the McPhersons moved ashore to the planned hotel site, so that Wally could attend school. Work began at the site on a cookhouse and bunkrooms, but things quickly started to go south. The investor passed away and his heirs had no interest in developing a resort on the shores of a remote desert lake.

With investor funds dried up, the McPherson's made a decision to scale back their plans. Instead of a health resort on the Island, they converted the completed bunkhouse and cookhouse on the mainland to a small hotel. Six additional rooms were added and the hotel was given the name the Mono Inn. The realignment of El Camino Sierra to just outside their backdoor gave hope to the McPhersons that their dreams of a health resort and large hotel would still someday achieve reality. They used the *Pahoa* to take guests and visitors on excursions out on Mono Lake.

But sometimes life happens. Wallis and Venita divorced in 1926. Venita kept the Mono Inn and the boat, and gained custody of young Wally. Through Venita's hard work, the Mono Inn became "the" gathering place on Mono Lake. In refute of Mark Twain's description of Mono Lake in his classic *Roughing It* where he referred to the Lake as a "solemn, sail-less sea...little graced with the picturesque...nothing that goes to make life desirable," Venita started "Mark Twain Days, which was held each August at the Mono Inn.

The festivities included a beauty contest, boat races, human and horse swimming races, and sack and foot races on shore. The day ended with a huge barbecue that attracted as many as 4,000 revelers. The event went a long way to dispel Twain's blasphemous comments.

Figure 84-Mark Twain Days featured a Miss Mono Beauty Pageant.

As years passed, Wally took on more and more responsibilities in running his mother's business. He especially enjoyed piloting the *Pahoa* on excursion trips on the Lake with the guests.

The *Pahoa* eventually fell victim to fire and was destroyed. But ever the optimist, Wally soon laid out the frame of a new boat and built this one on site at Mono Lake. The thirty-four-foot long by ten-foot wide vessel could carry 36 guests on trips out on the Lake and to its islands. The new boat was christened the *Venita* in honor of Wally's mother.

For a time during the 1940s and '50s, Mono Lake actually became somewhat popular with speed boaters. The Western Regional Championship Outdoor Regatta was held at Mono Lake. A marina was put in place on Mono Lake's southwest shore (now a Lake access point) to accommodate the number of boaters. Water skiers could be seen performing tricks on any given day during the summer.

Figure 85-The Mono Marina harbored an assortment of watercraft in the 50s & 60s.
But as L.A.'s diversions of Mono's water took place, the Lake's level dropped to a point that numerous hazards in the form of partially submerged tufa towers appeared. The salinity and saltiness of the Lake's waters also proved harsh on the boats and their motors. Boating on the Lake came to an end.

In 1994, the California State Water Resources Control Board ordered the Los Angeles Department of Water & Power to return and maintain the level of Mono Lake to a height necessary to maintain its ecological health. Since then, water being diverted to the City of L.A. has been greatly reduced. Hopefully, historic Mono Lake will still be a site to behold by travelers for many years to come as they make their way along the alluring roadway...known as El Camino Sierra.

CHAPTER THIRTY-TWO

I FEEL THE
EARTH MOVE

The dramatic scenery of the Eastern Sierra is enough to take one's breath away. As if the soaring heights of the Sierra Nevada to the west weren't enough, nature has provided mountains of almost equal stature to the east in the form of the Inyo and White Mountains. The Owens Valley has often been referred to as "Deepest Valley."

This kind of scenery doesn't happen by accident. Geologic processes have been at work for over 40-million years to create the landscape we see here today. One of these processes is called subduction, and is where one plate of the earth's crust is pushed below another. Where these two plates come together is a fault, and every time pressure is released along the fault, an earthquake occurs. There are several faults that occur in the Owens Valley.

In the early morning hours of March 26, 1872, the Owens Valley presented as peaceful a scene as eyes had ever looked upon, and the great mountains on either side appeared the very embodiment of solidity and stability. But at 2:25 a.m., a great rumbling and roaring from deep within the earth burst forth, followed by a tremendous shaking and rolling.

A huge earthquake had struck the Owens Valley, centered near the town of Lone Pine. Seismic measuring equipment had yet to be developed but geologists who have studied the quake have determined it was every bit as powerful as the great San Francisco earthquake of 1906. It's estimated the Lone Pine Earthquake (as it became known) would have measured 7.9 on the Richter scale.

Twenty-seven people died in the violent quake and at least another forty were injured. Fifty-two of the towns fifty-nine houses were destroyed. If there was a saving grace, it was that the area was still lightly populated in 1872. There were approximately 200 people in the Lone Pine area and only a few hundred more in the entire Valley at the time.

Figure 86-The Courthouse in Independence was badly damaged, along with scores of other buildings in Inyo County.

Vertical movement along the fault was 15 to 20 feet. Horizontal movement was a staggering 35 to 40 feet. The earth ruptured along this fault for a length of 85 miles. South of Lone Pine, 80 acre Diaz Lake was formed when the earth dropped 20 feet and opened up new springs that quickly filled the new depression.

The quake was felt as far as Red Bluff to the north, San Diego to the south and Elko, Nevada to the east. The same quake set off massive rockslides in Yosemite Valley, which were described in an eyewitness account by John Muir who was residing there at the time. Buildings were damaged or destroyed in every town in the Owens Valley.

Evidence of the huge fault scarp can still be clearly seen today. Visitors traveling on Whitney Portal Road should look for it about a mile west of its junction with El Camino Sierra, just after crossing over the L.A. Aqueduct.

CHAPTER THIRTY-THREE

SCIENCE AT EXTREME HEIGHTS

The White Mountains are yet another of those magical places that exist along the route of El Camino Sierra. White Mountain Peak, at 14,252 feet is not only the third highest peak in California; it is also the 13th highest in the United States outside Alaska. The views from its summit are among the best you can find. The ancient Bristlecone pines find the White Mountains quite to their liking, with the oldest specimen over 5,000 years old. The White Mountains are also home to the little known and highly esteemed White Mountain Research Center (WMRC.)

The WMRC is actually comprised of four separate locations. Crooked Creek Station at an elevation of 10,150 feet, Barcroft Station at 12,470 feet, Summit Hut located on the very summit of White Mountain Peak itself and Owens Valley Station located just outside the town of Bishop. WMRC is a unit of the University of California system and provides lodging, meals, labs and workspace to scientists and students from all over the world. It is also home of the University of California Los Angeles-Institute of Environment and Sustainability. The geologic exposure, steep topography, high elevation, arid climate, and potential for winter access make the center uniquely valuable for scientific study and education.

The first scientific research conducted in the "Whites" was done by the U.S. Navy shortly after the end of World War II. With the Cold War in full force, the Navy conducted classified and unclassified research at the Crooked Creek area in field-testing heat-seeking missiles. The Navy also conducted studies in astronomy, atmospheric physics and cosmic rays.

Professor Nello Pace from the University of California Berkley (UCB) saw an opportunity in the White Mountains to expand the University's research in a variety of fields including the effects of high altitude on living things. Professor Pace gained the support of UCB's administrators, and the University began conducting its own testing and research in 1950. The Navy ended their own testing at WMRC several years later.

WMRC was greatly expanded and the facilities improved upon over the next 30 years. Research at first was only conducted during the summer months, but modernization soon enabled researchers to conduct tests throughout the year.

The stations are closed to the public except for special public events and open houses. One can observe some of the facilities while hiking on the White Mountain Peak trail. Today, WMRC continues to provide numerous opportunities to scientists and students to conduct their research in this unique and unusual high alpine environment that looks peacefully down upon…El Camino Sierra.

Figure 87-(above) Barcroft Station has been in operation since the 1950s.
Figure 88-(below)- Summit Station sits atop White Mountain Pk.

CHAPTER THIRTY-FOUR

JEWEL OF
THE SIERRA

It's difficult to consider any one of the many scenic resorts, lodges, hotels and camps in the Eastern Sierra, as being "better" than any other. Each one has its own special uniqueness and attractiveness. They all have the commonality of having provided hundreds of thousands of weary city dwellers special lifetime lasting memories of their time along El Camino Sierra.

One mountain resort in particular ranks near the top of the list for both tenure and emotional ties. The first resort in Big Pine Canyon was started in the early 1900s. Simply known as "that place up Big Pine Canyon," it consisted of a few small cabins, a tiny hotel and a dining room. A few miles further up the trail at an elevation of 11,000 feet, lay a few tent cabins catering to hardy anglers dipping their line in the numerous nearby lakes.

As the story goes, a Big Pine lumberyard suffering the effects of a downturned economy sent employees with surplus lumber up Big Pine Canyon to make improvements to the camps and construct the most beautiful lodge of its kind in the Eastern Sierra.

The result of their work was named Glacier Lodge, and 5½-miles further by foot or horseback was Lake Camp. Glacier Lodge was a stately hostelry that was often described as a more affordable but equal in comfort alternative, to the fine European mountain resorts. For years, it promoted itself as being "The Nearest High Sierra Resort."

And despite its remote location, Lake Camp, located on the shore of Fourth Lake, offered nothing short of extremely comfortable "backcountry" accommodations. A 1940s-brochure boasted "Cabins, tent cabins and newly floored tents. Boats may be had at reasonable rates. Dining room and hot showers." It is interesting to note that the brochure also mentions that Walter Dow (Chapter 7) was the proprietor at that time.

Figure 89-(above) Glacier Lodge has welcomed guests since the 1920s.
Figure 90--(below) Lake Camp was located five and a half miles above Glacier
Lodge and featured tent cabins along with a sturdy built lodge.

Visitors were welcomed at Lake Camp by manager Belle Tyler for a
number of years. Tyler was known as a great cook, who could turn out
delicious sticky buns on a large woodstove. Not an easy feat-especially at
11,000-foot elevation. Belle also had the notoriety of staying at Lake Camp
most winters as its caretaker.

One Lodge owner named Pete Holms didn't have the best of relationships with the nearby Big Pine Pack Station's owner Ed Sargent. No one knows why the two men didn't like each other. Professional jealousy...differing concepts? One year, Holms got the idea that Lake Camp should have boats for its visitors to rent for fishing the lakes when they arrived at Lake Camp. He bought six 12-foot long boats that weighed 150-pounds each.

Holms asked Sargent if he could hire him to haul the boats up to Lake Camp with his mules. Sargent quoted the outrageous price of $125 for each boat! Holms and his partner said they would haul the boats up themselves. They fashioned wooden slings and proceeded to push, pull and drag three of the boats 5½ miles and 3,000 feet up to Lake Camp. Holms and Sargent finally agreed on $25 each, and the mules hauled the remaining three boats up the trail to Lake Camp.

The creation of first the High Sierra Primitive Area and later the John Muir Wilderness, forced the closure of Lake Camp and its demolition in 1963.

In 1929, Hollywood actor Lon Cheney obtained a special use permit from the U.S. Forest Service (USFS) to build a "modest" cabin a few miles above Glacier Lodge (and before Lake Camp). A road continued a few miles further up Big Pine Canyon than it does today, making it only a one and a half mile hike to his cabin site.

Cheney and his family had often camped and fished at the site along Big Pine Creek. The beautiful 1,300 square foot cabin had two-foot thick rock walls, tongue and groove pine floors and a huge granite fireplace. The home was designed by renowned African-American architect Paul Revere Williams.

Unfortunately, Cheney was able to enjoy his one-of-a-kind vacation home for only a few months before his sudden death in 1930. The home continued to be used by new owners up until 1980, when the USFS permit expired and the cabin and its land reverted to the Forest Service. Originally, it was planned for demolition but the Forest Service decided the amount of dynamite needed to destroy the sturdy structure would cause more damage to the surroundings than letting it stay. Today, the cabin remains in good shape and its exterior can be viewed by hikers on their way up the trail along the north fork of Big Pine Creek.

Glacier Lodge retained a loyal following of guests throughout the years. Over time, it became known as the "Jewel of the Sierra." Famed Sierra mountaineer Norman Clyde was Glacier's winter caretaker during the 1950s and '60s. In 1959 while Norman was briefly away, a huge snowfall buried Glacier Lodge, followed by an avalanche that literally sealed the building (and destroyed a few cabins). The end result was an enormous propane explosion was set off that destroyed the main Lodge building.

It was soon rebuilt but in 1998, Glacier Lodge suffered another mortal blow, this time at the hands of a fire. Plans to rebuild it again never came to bear. Today the current owners operate a small store, cafe and a few rustic cabins.

There are many tales from the Eastern Sierra that have seldom been told. Be sure and make time to stop and take in a few of the secrets from this, and all the magical and memorable places, as you make your way...along El Camino Sierra.

Figure 91-Glacier Lodge brochure circa 1950s.

CHAPTER THIRTY-FIVE

SKI INDEPENDENCE

Skiing and snowboarding are some of the most popular activities found along El Camino Sierra. Today, over one and a half million visitors enjoy Mammoth and June Mountain Ski areas each year.

These two world-class ski destinations have not always held a monopoly on the Eastern Sierra shredders. Over the years, skiers have made their way down the slopes of dozens of nearby slopes. In the 1960s, the U.S. Forest Service (U.S.F.S.) issued directives to their Forest Supervisors to come up with possible locations for ski developments on their managed lands.

In the Inyo National Forest alone, Trail Peak (see Chapter 18), Bishop Bowl, Red Mountain, Sherwin Bowl, McGee Mountain, Mt. Warren and Dunderberg Peak north of Conway Summit were all considered as possible sites for ski resorts. Sherwin Bowl south of Mammoth Lakes was still in the running to be developed as recently as the 1990s.

One area, not only had the full support and approval of the U.S.F.S, but also had a fully developed business plan including several dozen investors behind it.

Robinson Basin is the name given to the north facing slopes and bowls above Onion Valley, located 13 miles west of Independence. Mammoth Mountain founder Dave McCoy was known to have skied in the vicinity as early as 1935.

In 1938, Los Angeles Department of Water & Power hydrographer Vic Taylor began to test the Robinson Basin slopes on his boards. The steep slopes and good late season snow made the area very attractive for skiing. Taylor and his friends would use trucks jacked up with a rear tire removed as the first makeshift rope tows. As time progressed, portable rope tows replaced the jacked-up truck method.

Taylor and his friends continued to ski Robinson Basin and other areas along the Onion Valley Road for the next several years. He collaborated with Independence businesspersons O.K. and Anna Kelley to develop what became known first as the Inyo Ski Club and later the Onion Valley Ski Club.

Figure 92-Patches from two different Robinson Basin Ski Clubs.

Snow was not removed on the old Onion Valley Road during the winter months. Taylor, the Kellys and their friends would set up their portable rope tows as far as the snow depth would allow them to drive their vehicles. Popular spots for skiing were; above the Seven Pines summer home tract, Felman's Saddle, the second road crossing of Independence Creek and at road's end at Onion Valley/Robinson Basin itself.

The Robinson Basin area was fairly popular into the late 1950s, drawing not only the local folk from Independence and Lone Pine, but a fair number of southern Californians who would make their way north, especially to take advantage of the late season snow. Local schools had their own ski clubs, with many a young Southern Inyoite getting their first taste of downhill on the slopes above Independence.

In 1958, Big Bear Ski entrepreneur Tommi Tyndall thought he saw potential for a large destination ski resort at Robinson Basin and obtained a U.S.F.S. permit. He changed the name of the area to "Inyo Basin" and sent out a prospectus to primarily Independence and Lone Pine residents, offering them the "opportunity" to invest in his new Sierra ski resort.

Tyndall's plans called for three chair lifts with the highest one reaching an elevation of 12,490 feet, more than 1,400 feet higher than Mammoth Mountain's summit! Tyndall promised an "end of season" race scheduled for July 4th.

Figure 93-A portable rope tow was used wherever conditions would allow.

Figure 94-Artist's rendition of Tyndall's proposed Inyo Basin Ski Area.

Tyndall was heavily involved with his Big Bear operations and the proposed Inyo Basin development never came about, save for a warming hut that was also used as a small camp store in the summer months. Tyndall died in a snow grooming accident at Big Bear in 1964. Locals continued to operate the portable rope tows but the Forest Service began to phase out the permits to operate them, and skiing at Onion Valley soon came to an end. The camp store continued to operate until it was destroyed by a winter avalanche.

Today, the foundation of the warming hut is still clearly visible just north of the Onion Valley hiker parking area. The remains of a rope tow structure used at Felman's Saddle are also easy to spot.

So many hopes, so many dreams, found among the fertile fields of so many fond memories, here…along El Camino Sierra.

Figure 95-The ski hut at Onion Valley also served as a camp store in summer.

CHAPTER THIRTY-SIX

THE RED FISH

For decades, travelers who were headed to their favorite Eastern Sierra destination, were guided by the friendly and welcoming profile of the "Red Fish." Erected at numerous spots along El Camino Sierra, the Red Fish was the brainchild of yet another of the brilliant Inyo Good Roads Club's forward thinkers and promoters extraordinaire.

Lemoyne Hazard was an early member of the Inyo Good Roads Club. Hazard opened one of El Camino Sierra's first auto repair shops in Bishop. Knowing many of those who motored to the Eastern Sierra in those early days would greatly benefit from having as much information available as possible, Hazard posted hundreds of road signs in the shape of a big red fish, with the miles and distances to communities and destinations posted prominently upon them.

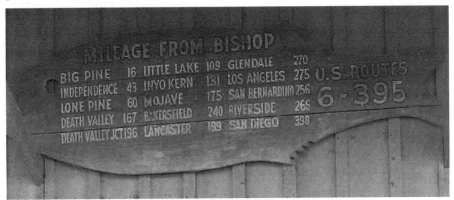

Figure 96-An original Red Fish mileage sign is on display at Laws Museum.

The promotion came to be known simply as the "Red Fish." The nation had its *Burma Shave* signs, El Camino Sierra had its *Red Fish*. Hazard was also an Inyo County Deputy Sheriff. He served his community diligently until he met his mortal fate while responding to a domestic disturbance in 1925. Lemoyne is one of five Inyo County law enforcement officers who have lost their life in the line of duty.

The Red Fish promotion was wildly successful. Travelers became as familiar with the crimson Pisces as they did with the silhouette of Mt. Whitney. Hazard's family not only continued the successful promotion after his death, they greatly expanded upon it as well. Decals were produced and tourists and locals alike would proudly display the Red Fish on their car's windows and bumpers.

Figure 97-Hazard's garage produced Red Fish decals in addition to the hundreds of Red Fish road signs they had posted along El Camino Sierra.

Figure 98-Hazard's garage in Bishop, with the iconic Red Fish signage prominently displayed (top left).

Beautify America programs eventually led to a dramatic decline in the number of signs posted along the nation's highways. The Eastern Sierra was no exception and the Red Fish signs soon became yet another fond memory...and true tale...found along El Camino Sierra.

EPILOGUE

We are mindful that this book would not have near the gravity it may have mustered if it were not for the delightful and enchanting photographs we have been so very fortunate to have assembled. The number of sources are many, and we are extremely grateful for them all. Had these photographers not taken the time to document and preserve these various moments in history and human enjoyment, this literary effort would simply not have been possible.

We feel it only fitting to conclude *Tales Along El Camino Sierra* with a brief reflection into the work of one legendary photographer, whose photo-postcards may have done more to promote the beauty and appeal of Inyo and Mono to the "outside" world than anything else.

Burton Frasher and his wife Josephine opened a photo studio in Laverne, California in 1914 (he later moved his studio to Pomona). Frasher figured he could make a living by taking photographs of outdoor scenes and publishing them as photo-postcards. Frasher's style was different from other photographers of his era. He incorporated the distant vista, the trail of footsteps, and the occasional human being in his photos, all methods to keep monumentality in perspective. Frasher covered a vast area of the American West, but he may be best known for his spectacular work in Eastern California.

We hope you enjoy a few of Burton's personal and reflective photo-postcards as a fitting final sunset on your journey along…El Camino Sierra.

With his son at Kearsarge

With son and wife at Sonora

At the end of another great day in the Eastern Sierra

Sunset on the desert...along El Camino

BIBLIOGRAPHY

Armstrong, Larry-Saga of Inyo County, 1977

Babb, Dave-Fish Planting in the Eastern Sierra, Oct-1989

Banta & Carle, Don & David-Mono Lake Basin, 2008

Brierly, A.A.-Inyo Independent, March 17, 1977

Brooks, Joan-The Desert Padre, 1997

Brown, Brian-Personal Notes, Mar-2015

Chaffey, George-Personal Letter to Owens Valley Improvement Company
Board of Directors   May 16, 1912

Chalfant, Willie-The Story of Inyo, 1922

Chalfant, Willie-Inyo Register, December 30, 1920

Chalfant, Willie-Inyo Register, Oct 6, 1910

Chalfant, Willie Inyo Register, June 16, 1921

Coe, Ted-The News Review, April 24, 1921

Datin, Richard-Inyo Independent, July 7, 1977

DeLea, Ray-http://www.owensvalleyhistory.com/

Dent, Jim-Personal Memoirs, Apr-1971

Deutsche, Craig-Desert Report-Pioneers in the Desert, Aug-1914

Dow, Walter-Personal Correspondence , Oct 29, 1963

Edmiston, Beula-Committee for the Preservation of the Tule Elk Newsletter,
Nov 15, 1965

Garrigues, George-The Album-Aeroplane Conquers Mt. Whitney Oct-1989

Geltner, Ted-Inyo Register, July 22, 1992

Glasscock, Harry-Owens Valley Herald, May 12, 1920

Gracey, Robert-Oral Interview , Jul-2016

Hamilton, Russ-Oral Interview , Dec-2016

Hart, Alan District Engineer-California Department of Transportation District
IX-The Story of District IX, 1951-1953

Holland, Howard-Oral Interview, Dec-2016

Ivey, Elsie-Oral Interview, Dec-2016

Ivey, Bruce-Oral Interview , Apr-2016

Jenkins, Marguerite-Desert Magazine-Dirty Sock, Apr-1960

Jones, Rufus-The American Friend, January 1900

Kruse, John-http://www.ghosttowns.com/states/nv/aurora.html

Kyne, Peter-Sunset Magazine-Two Mules and a Motorist, Aug-1912

Leggett, Thomas-Twelfth Report of the State Mineralogist, Sept. 1894

Livermont, Kirk-http://www.livermont.com

Lukins, Julian-Inyo Register, June 13, 1999

Maravelas, Mark-Oral Interview, Dec. 2016

Martin, Emile-The Album-Chalfant Publishing

Meeman, Edward-The Pittsburgh Press, April 16, 1965

Messick, Tim-https://bodiehillsplants.com/tag/green-creek/

Mich'l, Devon-http://www.aaroads.com/blog/2010/07/25/the-midland-trail/

Morning, Robin-Tracks of Passion, 2008

Mullholland, C.-The Historical Society of Southern California, Vol 3, No. 2 1894

Packwood, Dave-Westways-Wedding of the Waters, Dec-1937

Pavlick, Robert-Norman Clyde: Legendary Mountaineer of California's Sierra Nevada, 2008

Pister, Phil-Outdoor California-Summer in the Sierra, Sep-1965

Pritchett, Daniel-http://www.wmrc.edu/

Reynolds, Dave-Inyo Register, March 7, 1998

Roeser, Marye-http://www.mulemuseum.org/the-mount-whitney-trail.html

Rose, Gene-Yosemite's Tioga Country, 2006

Sorrells, Susan-Personal Notes, Mar-2015

Staff, USFS-Horseshoe Meadows Land Use Plan, 1974

Stump, Al -The Herald Examiner, Nov 23, 1969

Taylor, Marie-The Album-Chalfant Publishing, Volume 11 # 1

Thomas, C.R.-Owens Valley Improvement Company-Marketing Brochure

Thorsoh, Oliver-Personal Letter to Dorothy Cragen, Nov 14, 1964

Tirock, Jim-https://cinetrains.wordpress.com/2012/01/13/the-black-widow-of-black-rock-southern-pacific-in-bad-day-at-black-rock/

Unknown, Author-http://www.merrell-wolff.org/

Unknown, Author-William Penn Colonial Association Investment Pamphlet, 1902

Unknown, Author-Inyo Independent, Sep. 9, 1910

Unknown, Author-Inyo Register, Apr. 13, 1922

Unknown, Author-Owens Valley Herald, Nov. 12, 1919

Unknown, Author-Inyo Register, Dec. 25, 1991

Unknown, Author-Inyo Independent, Mar. 23, 1934

Unknown, Author-Sierra Club Bulletin-Trout Planting

Unknown, Author-San Francisco Call, Jul. 7, 1912

Unknown, Author-San Francisco Call, Jul. 14, 1912

Unknown, Author-Sacramento Union, Jun. 6, 1912

Unknown, Author-Motor West Magazine, Apr. 15, 1921

Unknown, Author-Biographical Profile of Franklin-Merrell-Wolff

Unknown, Author-Inyo Independent, Apr. 19, 1973

Unknown, Author-The Whittier Daily News, Jan-1965

Unknown, Author-Inyo Independent, June 11, 1909

Unknown, Author-Inyo Independent, June 18, 1909

Unknown, Author-Manzanar Commercial Club, 2008

Unknown, Author-Manzanar Fruit & Canning Company-Articles of Incorporation, May 29, 1919

Unknown, Author-http://lonepinechamber.org/history/mt-whitney-history, Mar-2015

Unknown, Author-Mt Whitney-Death Valley Highway Celebration-Program, Oct-1937

Unknown, Author-Mono County Historical Society Newsletter, Jun-2005

Unknown, Author-http://www.monolake.org/mlc/

Unknown, Author-https://carsoncolorado.com/

Unknown, Author-http://www.keoughshotsprings.com/history.html

Vaughn, Pam-Correspondence, Dec-2016

Von Blon, John-Los Angeles Times, Nov-1959

Warren, George-Personal Letter, Jun-1929

Weiser, Kathy-http://www.legendsofamerica.com/ca-treasures8.html

Williams, Ted-http://ted-ology.blogspot.com/

IMAGES

El Camino Sierra Map-Author's Collection
El Camino Sierra Official Dedication
El Camino Sierra along Mono Lake-Eastern California Museum
Figure 1- Copyright 1910 California Department of Transportation, all rights reserved
Figure 2-Drawn by W.G. Scott, Inyo Good Roads Cub-Author's Collection
Figure 3-Eastern California Museum
Figure 4-Eastern California Museum
Figure 5-Courtesy Ray DeLea www.owensvalleyhistory.com
Figure 5A- Copyright 1910 California Department of Transportation, all rights reserved
Figure 6-Eastern California Museum
Figure 7-Eastern California Museum
Figure 8-Eastern California Museum
Figure 9-Eastern California Museum
Figure 10-Eastern California Museum
Figure 10A-Eastern California Museum
Figure 11-Library of Congress
Figure 12-Copyright 1910 California Department of Transportation, all rights reserved
Figure 12A-Library of Congress
Figure 13-Thomas Photograph, Bishop, CA
Figure 14-Eastern California Museum
Figure-15 Eastern California Museum
Figure 16-Eastern California Museum
Figure 17-Eastern California Museum
Figure 18-Eastern California Museum
Figure 19-Eastern California Museum
Figure 20-Eastern California Museum
Figure 21-Eastern California Museum
Figure 22-San Diego Air & Space Museum
Figure 23-Eastern California Museum
Figure 23A-Eastern California Museum
Figure 24-Franklin Merrell-Wolff Fellowship
Figure 25-Author's Collection
Figure 26-Author's Collection
Figure 27-Author's Collection
Figure 28-Eastern California Museum

Figure 29-Courtesy Brian Brown
Figure 30-Author's Collection
Figure 31-Eastern California Museum
Figure 32-Courtesy Friends of the Mt. Whitney Fish Hatchery
Figure-32A-Courtesy Friends of the Mt. Whitney Fish Hatchery
Figure 33-Author's Collection
Figure 34-Patrick Poendl
Figure 35-Eastern California Museum
Figure 36-Internet Movie Cars Database
Figure 37-Eastern California Museum
Figure 38-Eastern California Museum
Figure 39-Eastern California Museum
Figure 40-Authors Collection
Figure 41-Author's Collection
Figure 42-Eastern California Museum
Figure 43-Eastern California Museum
Figure 44-Eastern California Museum
Figure 45-Eastern California Museum
Figure 46-Eastern California Museum
Figure 47-Eastern California Museum
Figure 48-Eastern California Museum
Figure 49-Authors Collection
Figure 50-Author's Collection
Figure 51-Painting by William McKeever, Eastern California Museum
Figure 52-Courtesy Ray DeLea www.owensvalleyhistory.com
Figure 53-Thomas Photography, Bishop, CA
Figure 54-Eastern California Museum
Figure 55-Terrance Emerson, tntemerson.com
Figure 56-Eastern California Museum
Figure 57-Radomír Režný
Figure 58-Photograph by US Navy, courtesy Mono Basin Historical Society
Figure 60-Courtesy Thomas Photography, Bishop, CA
Figure 61-Eastern California Museum
Figure 62-Eastern California Museum
Figure 63-Climbing Magazine, Author's Collection-
Figure 64-Photo by Burton Frasher, Eastern California Museum
Figure 65-Photo by Burton Frasher, Eastern California Museum
Figure 66-Eastern California Museum
Figure 67-Eastern California Museum
Figure 68-Carson & Colorado Railway
Figure 69-https://cinetrains.wordpress.com

Figure 70-Author's Collection
Figure 71-Eastern California Museum
Figure 72-Eastern California Museum
Figure 73-Author's Collection
Figure 74-Eastern California Museum
Figure 75-Eastern California Museum
Figure 76-Photo by Burton Frasher, Eastern California Museum
Figure 77-Eastern California Museum
Figure 78-Eastern California Museum
Figure 79-Inyo Register
Figure 80-www.aaroads.com
Figure 81-https://bodiehillsplants.com/ Tim Messick
Figure 82-https://bodiehillsplants.com/ Tim Messick
Figure 83-Courtesy Mono Basin Historical Society
Figure 84-Eastern California Museum
Figure 85-Mono Basin Historical Society
Figure 86-Eastern California Museum
Figure 87-Courtesy White Mountain Research Center
Figure 88-Author's Collection
Figure 89-Photo by Burton Frasher, Eastern California Museum
Figure 90-Photo by Burton Frasher, Eastern California Museum
Figure 91-Eastern California Museum
Figure 92-Courtesy Robert Gracey
Figure 93-Courtesy Robert Gracey
Figure 94-Courtesy Robert Gracey
Figure 95-Courtesy Robert Gracey
Figure 96-Author's collection
Figure 97-Eastern California Museum
Figure 98-Courtesy Pam Vaughn-Laws Museum, Bishop, CA
Epilogue-All four photographs by Burton Frasher

If you have a comment you would like to send us, please do so! You can reach us at
elcaminosierra395@gmail.com
or
Woodruff   1326 Kimmerling Rd # A Gardnerville, NV 89460
Thank you and we hope you have enjoyed
Tales Along El Camino Sierra.

Made in the USA
Columbia, SC
01 June 2019